Collins Junior World A...

Editorial advisor **Dr. Stephen Scoffham**

Contents

2 What is an atlas?

Globes

Globes are models of the earth. They show the true shape and size of the continents.

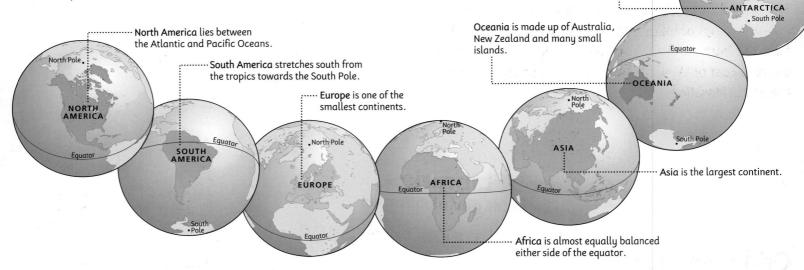

North Pole

North America lies between the Atlantic and Pacific Oceans.

NORTH AMERICA

Equator

South America stretches south from the tropics towards the South Pole.

SOUTH AMERICA

Equator

South Pole

North Pole

Europe is one of the smallest continents.

EUROPE

Equator

North Pole

AFRICA

Equator

Africa is almost equally balanced either side of the equator.

North Pole

ASIA

Equator

Asia is the largest continent.

Oceania is made up of Australia, New Zealand and many small islands.

OCEANIA

Equator

South Pole

Antarctica encircles the South Pole.

Equator

ANTARCTICA

South Pole

Mapping the world

To show the world on a flat map we need to peel the surface of the globe and flatten it out. There are many different methods of drawing atlas maps. These methods are called **projections**.

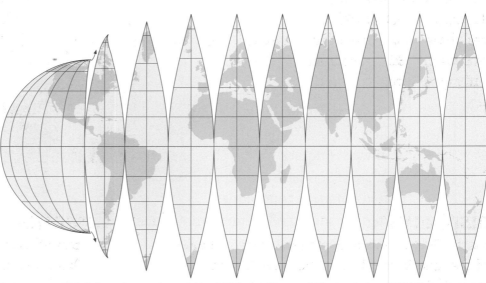

This is how the earth would look if the surface could be peeled and laid flat.

Projections

Map projections change the shape and size of the continents and oceans. The projection used for world maps in this atlas is called Eckert IV.

How the world map looks, depends on which continents are at the centre of the map. Compare the shape of Africa on the maps below to that on the globe.

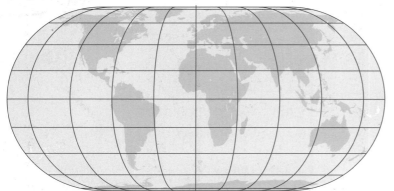

For UK atlases the world would look like this.

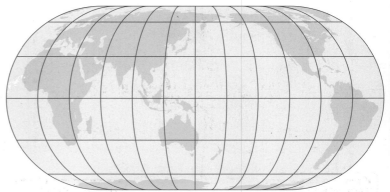

For Australian atlases the world would look like this.

Latitude and longitude

We use latitude and longitude to locate places on the earth's surface. Lines of **latitude** are imaginary lines. They are numbered in degrees North or South of the equator. Lines of **longitude** are imaginary lines which run from the North to the South Poles. They are numbered in degrees East or West of a line through London known as the Prime Meridian.

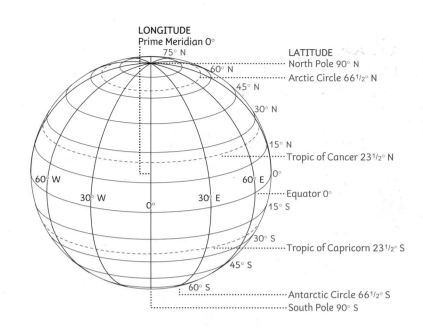

Grid references

Lines of latitude and longitude are used in this atlas to make a grid. The columns are labelled with a letter and the rows with a number. The grid code e.g. B6 can be used to find all places within one grid square.

Cartagena is in B8
Bogota is in B7
Piura is in A6

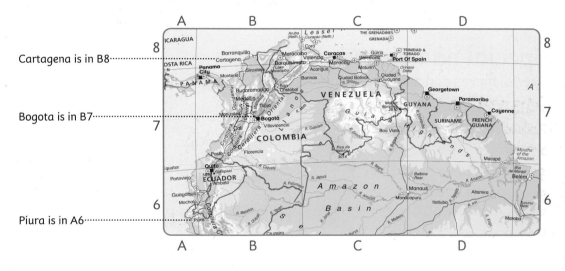

Hemispheres

The equator divides the globe into two halves. All land north of the equator is called the northern hemisphere. Land south of the equator is called the southern hemisphere. 0° and 180° lines of longitude also divide the globes into two imaginary halves, the western and eastern hemispheres.

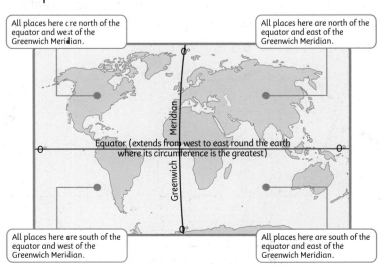

All places here are north of the equator and west of the Greenwich Meridian.

All places here are north of the equator and east of the Greenwich Meridian.

Equator (extends from west to east round the earth where its circumference is the greatest)

All places here are south of the equator and west of the Greenwich Meridian.

All places here are south of the equator and east of the Greenwich Meridian.

Direction

On most atlas maps you will find a compass. It shows the four compass points North (N), East (E), South (S) and West (W). These help us give more accurate directions.

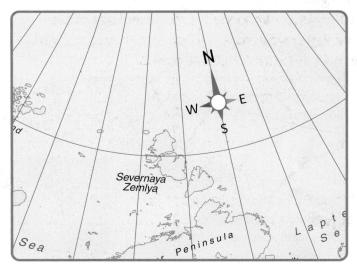

On atlas maps the north point always follows a line of longitude.

4 What is an atlas?

Atlas maps

Atlas maps tell us about the various parts of the world. They tell us about different environments in the world.

Some maps show country shapes and where towns are located within the country. These are called political maps.

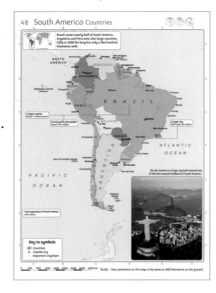

Some maps show landscapes. They show the physical environment.

Special names and numbers

Special names and numbers are used to label parts of an atlas map.

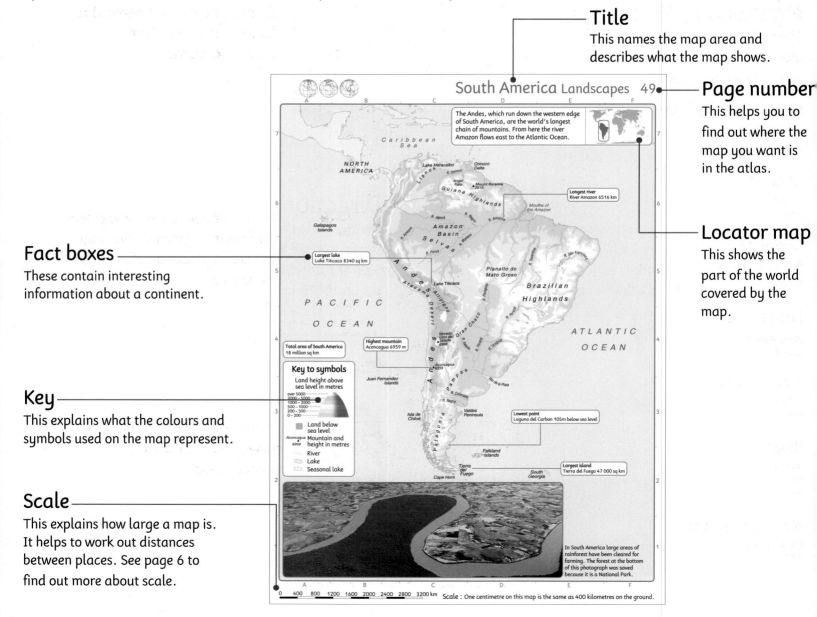

Title
This names the map area and describes what the map shows.

Page number
This helps you to find out where the map you want is in the atlas.

Locator map
This shows the part of the world covered by the map.

Fact boxes
These contain interesting information about a continent.

Key
This explains what the colours and symbols used on the map represent.

Scale
This explains how large a map is. It helps to work out distances between places. See page 6 to find out more about scale.

Map symbols

Maps are made up of symbols and names. The symbols can be points, lines or area colours.
A map is complete when the symbols and the names are combined.

Point symbols

- ■ Town stamps
- ▲ Mountain peaks
- ⊕ Airports

Lines

—— Roads   ---- Railways
—— Country boundaries
—— Rivers and canals
—— Coastline

Area colours

▢ Lake/sea

Land height above sea level in metres

over 5000 ············
3000 – 5000 ············
2000 – 3000 ············
1000 – 2000 ············
500 – 1000 ············
200 – 500 ············
0 – 200 ············

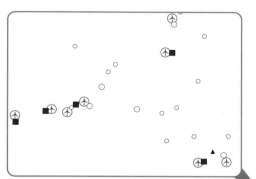

Point symbols are used on a map to show towns, mountain peaks and airports.

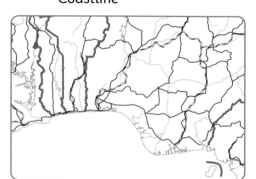

Lines are used on a map to show communications and drainage.

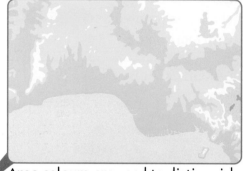

Area colours are used to distinguish the land from the sea and land height above sea level.

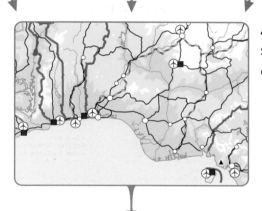

All the symbols are combined to show features and their correct locations.

Names on atlas maps

The style and size of the type used on maps helps to explain what the name means.

Large bodies of water

PACIFIC OCEAN
Gulf of Guinea

Islands

Cuba
Bioco

Countries

N I G E R I A
BENIN

Large cities

Porto-Novo
Lomé

Small towns

Parakou
Warri

Rivers

Mississippi
Nile
Amazon

Mountain peaks

Mount Cameroon
Everest

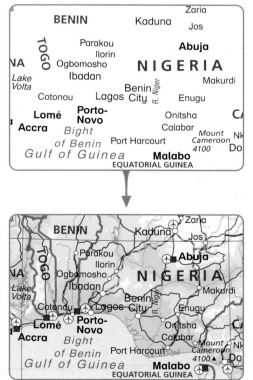

Names are needed to show places and features shown on the map. Only some places and features are named.

The map is complete when the symbols and the names are combined.

Scale

Maps are much smaller than the regions they show. To
compare the real area with the mapped area you have
to use a scale. Each map in this atlas shows its scale.
This is shown using a scale bar which is explained in words.

E.g.
```
0    200   400   600   800 km
```

Scale : One centimetre on this map is the same as 200 kilometres on the ground.

Large scale maps show smaller areas with more detail.

LARGE SCALE

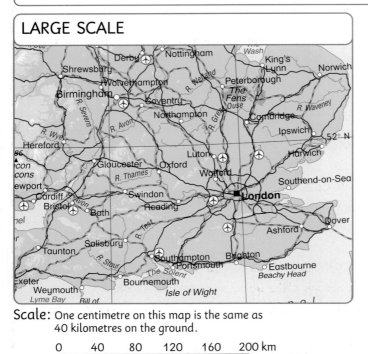

Scale: One centimetre on this map is the same as
40 kilometres on the ground.

```
0     40    80    120   160   200 km
```

MEDIUM SCALE

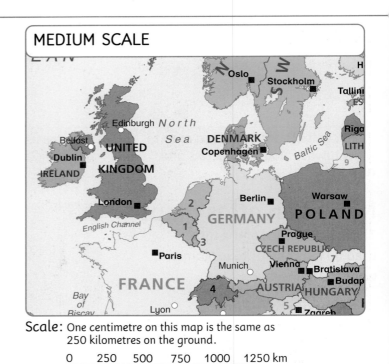

Scale: One centimetre on this map is the same as
250 kilometres on the ground.

```
0     250   500   750   1000  1250 km
```

Measuring distance

The scale of a map can be used to measure how far it is
between two places. For example, the straight line distance
between Boa Vista and Cayenne on the map to the right is
5 centimetres.

Look at the ruler.
One centimetre on this map is the same as 200 kilometres on
the ground. The real distance between Boa Vista and Cayenne
is therefore 1000 kilometres (i.e. 5 X 200).

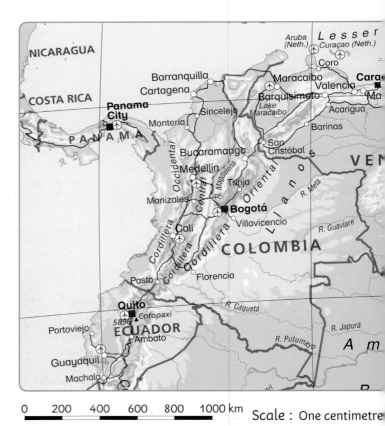

```
0    200   400   600   800   1000 km
```
Scale : One centimetre

Small scale maps show larger areas with less detail.

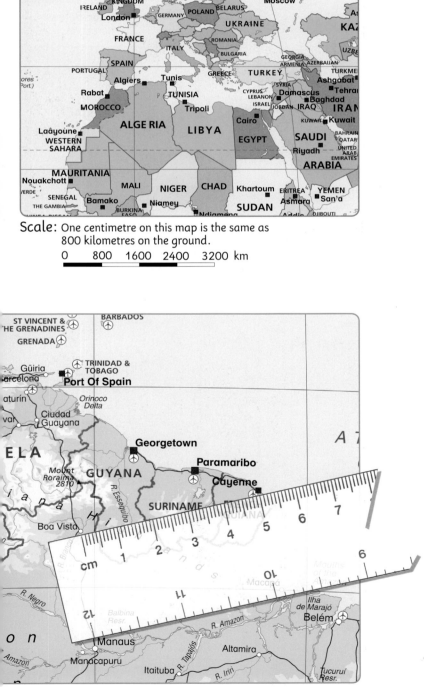

SMALL SCALE

Scale: One centimetre on this map is the same as 800 kilometres on the ground.

0   800   1600   2400   3200 km

...s map is the same as 200 kilometres on the ground.

Extend your knowledge and understanding by visiting these websites which provide lots of information and material to help with your homework and projects.

Places
European Union europa.eu/abc/
CIA Factbook www.cia.gov/cia/publications/factbook
Visit Britain www.visitbritain.com
Kids web Japan web-japan.org/kidsweb

Climate
Weather in the UK and abroad www.bbc.co.uk/weather
World climate statistics www.worldclimate.com
Climate change www.greenpeace.org.uk/climate

Population
World Population Prospects esa.un.org/unpp

Geography
National Geographic kids.nationalgeographic.com
Royal Geographical Society www.rgs.org

Mountains and rivers
Mountains of the world www.peakware.com
Rivers and coasts www.bbc.co.uk/schools/riversandcoasts

Maps and satellite images
Google Earth www.google.com/earth
Earth Observatory earthobservatory.nasa.gov
Ordnance Survey mapzone.ordnancesurvey.co.uk

International organizations
United Nations www.cyberschoolbus.un.org
The Commonwealth www.youngcommonwealth.org
Oxfam www.oxfam.org.uk/coolplanet/kidsweb
ActionAid International www.actionaid.org
Christian Aid www.christianaid.org.uk/resources/games
UNICEF www.unicef.org
Save the Children www.savethechildren.org

Environment
Greenpeace www.greenpeace.org.uk
World Wide Fund for Nature www.wwf.org.uk
Fairtrade www.fairtrade.org.uk
Recyclezone www.recyclezone.org.uk
Eco Friendly Kids www.ecofriendlykids.co.uk

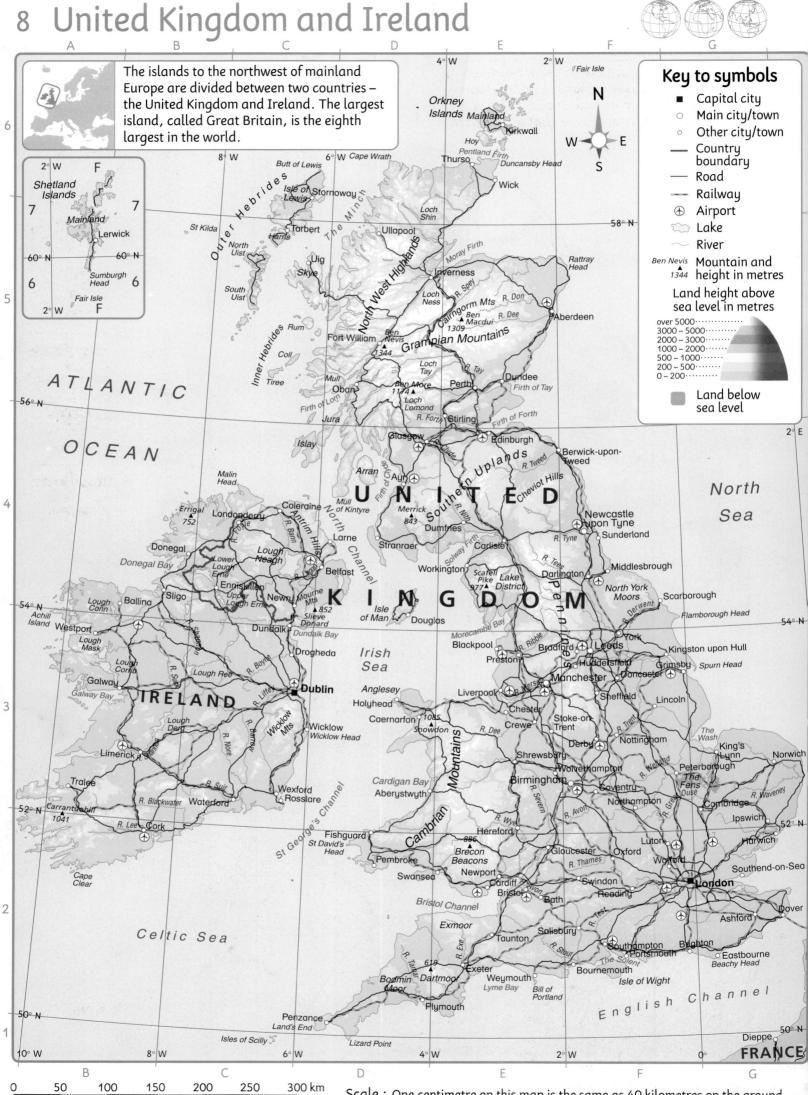

The islands to the northwest of mainland Europe are divided between two countries – the United Kingdom and Ireland. The largest island, called Great Britain, is the eighth largest in the world.

Key to symbols

- ■ Capital city
- ○ Main city/town
- ○ Other city/town
- —— Country boundary
- —— Road
- ---- Railway
- ⊕ Airport
- Lake
- River
- ▲ Ben Nevis 1344 Mountain and height in metres

Land height above sea level in metres

| over 5000 |
| 3000 – 5000 |
| 2000 – 3000 |
| 1000 – 2000 |
| 500 – 1000 |
| 200 – 500 |
| 0 – 200 |

Land below sea level

Scale : One centimetre on this map is the same as 40 kilometres on the ground.

0 50 100 150 200 250 300 km

Four countries make up the United Kingdom or UK. They are England, Scotland, Wales and Northern Ireland. The Isle of Man and Channel Islands are also part of the UK but have their own laws.

Key to symbols

- Countries
- ■ Capital city
- ● National capital
- ○ Important city/town

United Kingdom

Scotland

Northern Ireland

Wales

England

Ireland

ATLANTIC OCEAN

Shetland Islands

Orkney Islands

Outer Hebrides

Inverness

Aberdeen

Fort William

SCOTLAND

Dundee

North Sea

Glasgow   **Edinburgh**

Londonderry
NORTHERN IRELAND   **Belfast**

Newcastle upon Tyne

Middlesbrough

UNITED

IRELAND

Isle of Man

York

Dublin ■

Irish Sea

Blackpool   Bradford   Leeds
Preston

Manchester
Liverpool   Sheffield

KINGDOM

Stoke-on-Trent   Derby   Nottingham

ENGLAND   Norwich

Wolverhampton   Leicester
Birmingham
Coventry

WALES   Cambridge
Ipswich

Oxford

Swansea   **London** ■   Southend-on-Sea

Cardiff   Bristol   Reading   BELGIUM

Southampton   Brighton
Portsmouth
Bournemouth

Plymouth   Torquay

English Channel

Channel Islands   **FRANCE**

The UK government makes laws in the Houses of Parliament in London.

| | 50 | 100 | 150 | 200 | 250 | 300 km |

Scale : One centimetre on this map is the same as 50 kilometres on the ground.

The Scottish highlands are the emptiest part of the UK. There are many small islands around the coast. They are linked to the mainland by ferry.

Scotland has many mountains. Those which are over 3000 feet (914 m) high are called Munros. This one is in Glen Coe near Ben Nevis.

Key to symbols

○ Main city/town
○ Other city/town
— Road
╪ Railway
✈ Airport
Lake
River
Ben Nevis ▲ 1344 Mountain and height in metres

Land height above sea level in metres

over 1500
1000 – 1500
900 – 1000
500 – 900
200 – 500
100 – 200
0 – 100

N
W E
S

ATLANTIC OCEAN

Flannan Isles

Outer Hebrides

Butt of Lewis
Port of Ness
Tolsta Head

Great Bernera
Stornoway
Port Nan Giùran
Eye Peninsula

Lewis
Loch Langavat
Kebock Head

Scarp

Clishham 799
Tarbert
Scalpay

St Kilda

Harris

Pabbay
Berneray
Sound of Harris
Rodel

Rubha Hunish

Monach Islands

Lochmaddy
North Uist

Loch Snizort
Uig

The Storr 719

Little Minch

Benbecula

Dunvegan
Portree
Raasay

South Uist
Beinn Mhor 620

Skye

Cuillin Hills 993 928
Sgurr Alasdair Blaven
Scalpay

Lochboisdale

Sound of Barra
Eriskay

Soay
Ardvasar

Barra
Sheabhal 383
Castlebay
Vatersay
Sandray

Canna

Cuillin Sound

Rum
Askival 812

Inner Hebrides

Mingulay

Muck

Point of Ardnamurchan

Ben Hogh 104
Coll
Tobermory
Arinagour

Tiree
Scarinish

Loch Frisa

Eigg

Sound of Arisaig

Mallaig

Cape Wrath
Durness
Kinlochbervie
Foinaven 915
Handa Island
Scourie

The Minch

Point of Stoer
Lochinver
Loch Assynt
Ben More Assynt 998

Summer Isles

Ullapool
Loch Broom

An Teallach 1062
Fionn Loch

Rubha Reidh
Gairloch
Loch Ewe
Loch Maree

Sgurr Mor 1110

WESTER ROSS

L. Torridon
Rona
Inner Sound

R. Orrin
Sgurr a'Choire G. 1083
Loch Monar

Kyle of Lochalsh
Kyleakin

Carn Eighe 1183
Glen Affric

North West Highlands

Glen Shiel
Loch Cluanie
R. Moriston
Augus

Loch Hourn
Sound of Sleat
Ladhar Bheinn 1020

Loch Quoich
R. Garry
Loch Garry
Glen Garry

Loch Morar
Gulvain 983
Loch Arkaig
Loch Lochy

Sgurr Dhomhnuill 888

Fort William
1344
Ben Nevis

Loch Shiel
Loch Leven
Glen Coe

Loch Sunart
Morvern
Bidean nam Bian 1150

Lochaline
Loch Linnhe
Loch Etive

Sound of Mull

Scale : One centimetre on this map is the same as 12.5 kilometres on the ground.

0   25   50   75 km

4° W 3° W 2° W

Fair Isle

Papa Westray
Westray
N. Ronaldsay
North Ronaldsay
N. Ronaldsay Firth
Eday
Sanday
Rousay
Stronsay
Brough Head
Orkney Islands
Stronsay Firth
Shapinsay
Loch of Harray
Kirkwall
Stromness
Mainland
Skaill
Ward Hill 479
Scapa Flow
Hoy
Flotta
Burray
South Ronaldsay
Burwick
59° N

Pentland Firth

Dunnet Head
Thurso B.
John o'Groats
Duncansby Head
Dounreay
Thurso
Bettyhill
Loch Watten
R. Wick
Sinclair's Bay
Tongue
Loch Loyal
CAITHNESS
Wick
ERLAND
Loch Rimsdale
961 Ben Klibreck
R. Thurso
Lybster
R. Helmsdale
Lairg
R. Brora
Helmsdale
Brora
Golspie
Dornoch Firth
Tarbat Ness
Tain
Invergordon
Cromarty Firth
Moray Firth
Lossiemouth
Cullen
Macduff
Fraserburgh
Buckie
Banff
Black Isle
Elgin
Fochabers
Turriff
Crimond
Rattray Head
Dingwall
Fortrose
Nairn
Forres
Knock Hill
R. Deveron
Mintlaw
Conon Bridge
Moray Firth
Keith
R. Isla 430
Rothes
Peterhead
Beauly
Inverness
Dufftown
Huntly
Cruden Bay
R. Findhorn
R. Ness
R. Nairn
Strathspey
STRATHBOGIE
R. Ythan
Ellon
Loch Ness
Grantown-on-Spey
R. Bogie
Oldmeldrum
Inverurie
Aviemore
R. Avon
R. Don
Kintore
Dyce
SCOTLAND
adhlaith Mountains
Cairn Gorm 1245
Cairngorm Mts
Aberdeen
Kingussie
Ben Macdui 1309
Newtonmore
Aboyne
R. Dee
Banchory
R. Spey
Braemar
Grampian Mountains
1155
Ballater
R. Dee
Dalwhinnie
Lochnagar
North R. Esk
Stonehaven
Loch Ericht
Carn nan Gabhar 1121
Glenshee
Inverbervie
en der
L. Rannoch
Blair Atholl
South R. Esk
Backwater Reservoir
Laurencekirk
rampian Mountains
1082
Loch Tummel
Pitlochry
R. Isla
Brechin
R. Tay
Schiehallion
R. Tummel
Kirriemuir
Montrose
noch or
R. Lyon
Strathmore
Ben Lawers 1214
Aberfeldy
Blairgowrie
Coupar Angus
Sidlaw Hills
Forfar
Arbroath
Carnoustie

NORTH SEA

58° N

G 2° W H I 1° W

Herma Ness
Unst
Point of Fethaland
Yell Sound
Fetlar
Ronas Hill 450
Yell
Toft
Out Skerries
St. Magnus Bay
Muckle Roe
Mainland
Papa Stour
Whalsay
Foula
Shetland Islands
Silom Voe
Lerwick
Bressay
60° N

Sumburgh
Sumburgh Head

Fair Isle
4 G 2° W H 1° W I

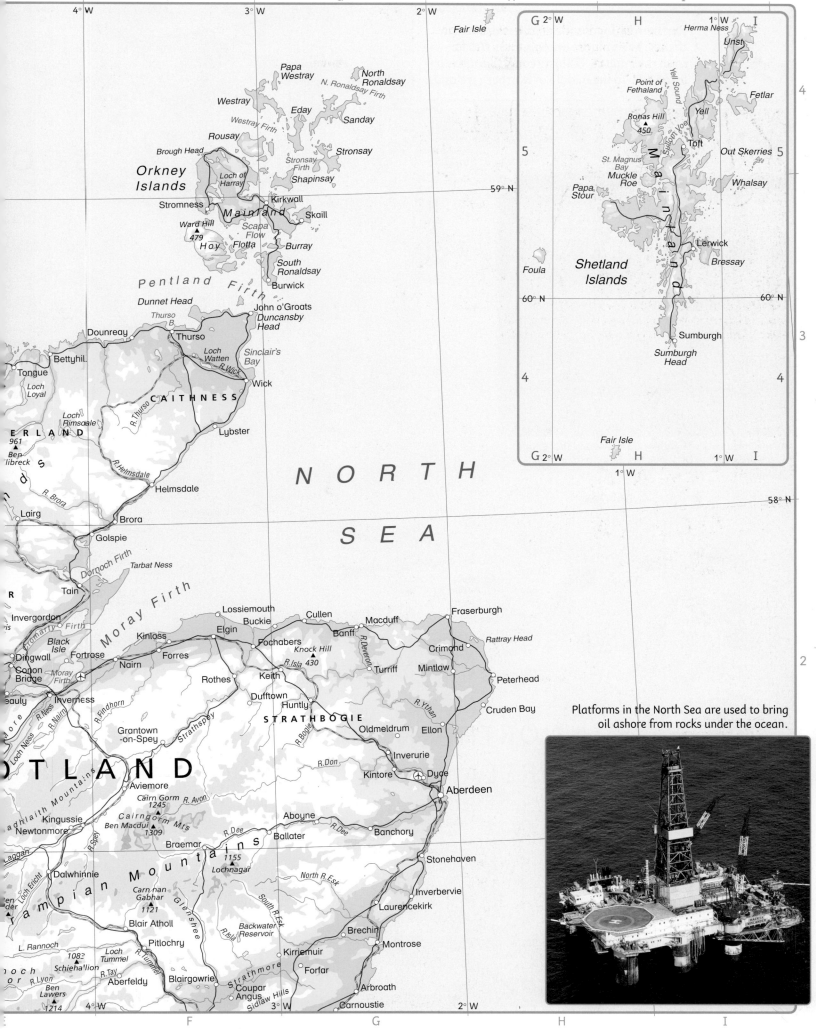

Platforms in the North Sea are used to bring oil ashore from rocks under the ocean.

Northern Ireland is the smallest country in the UK. Most places are less than 100 km from the capital, Belfast. Lough Neagh is a large lake in the middle of Northern Ireland.

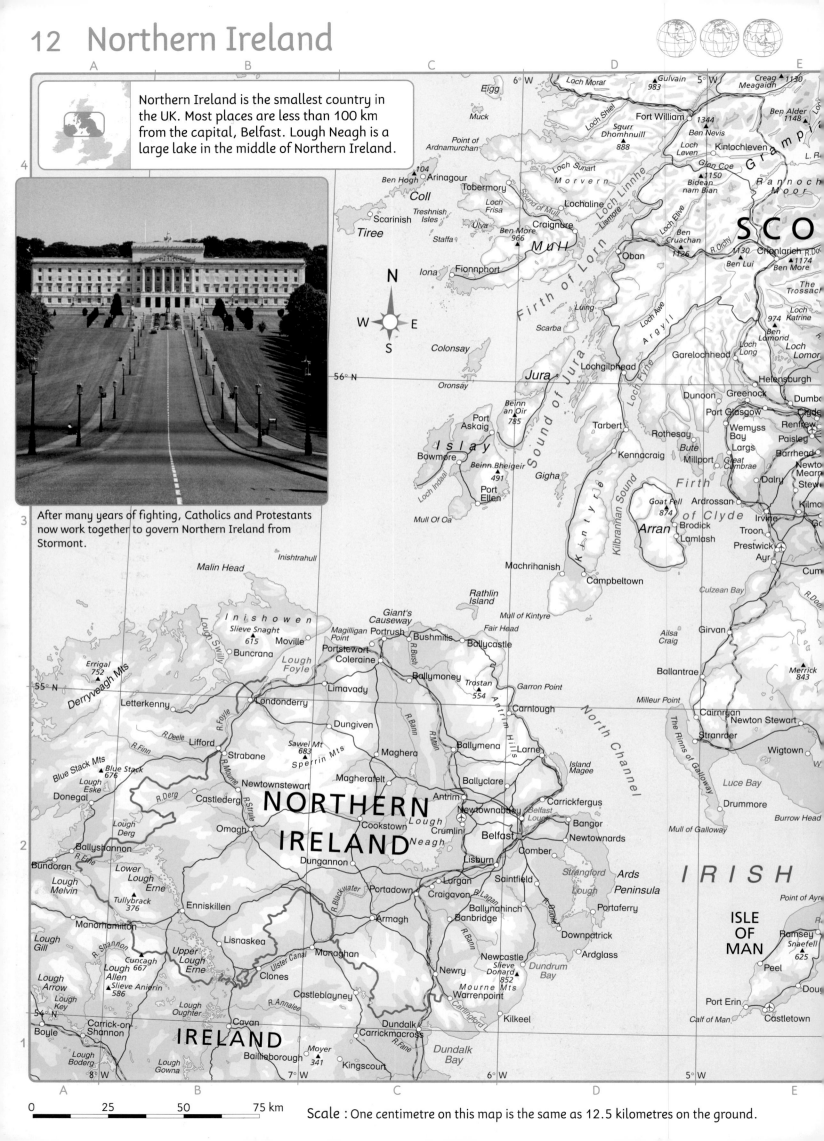

After many years of fighting, Catholics and Protestants now work together to govern Northern Ireland from Stormont.

0   25   50   75 km

Scale : One centimetre on this map is the same as 12.5 kilometres on the ground.

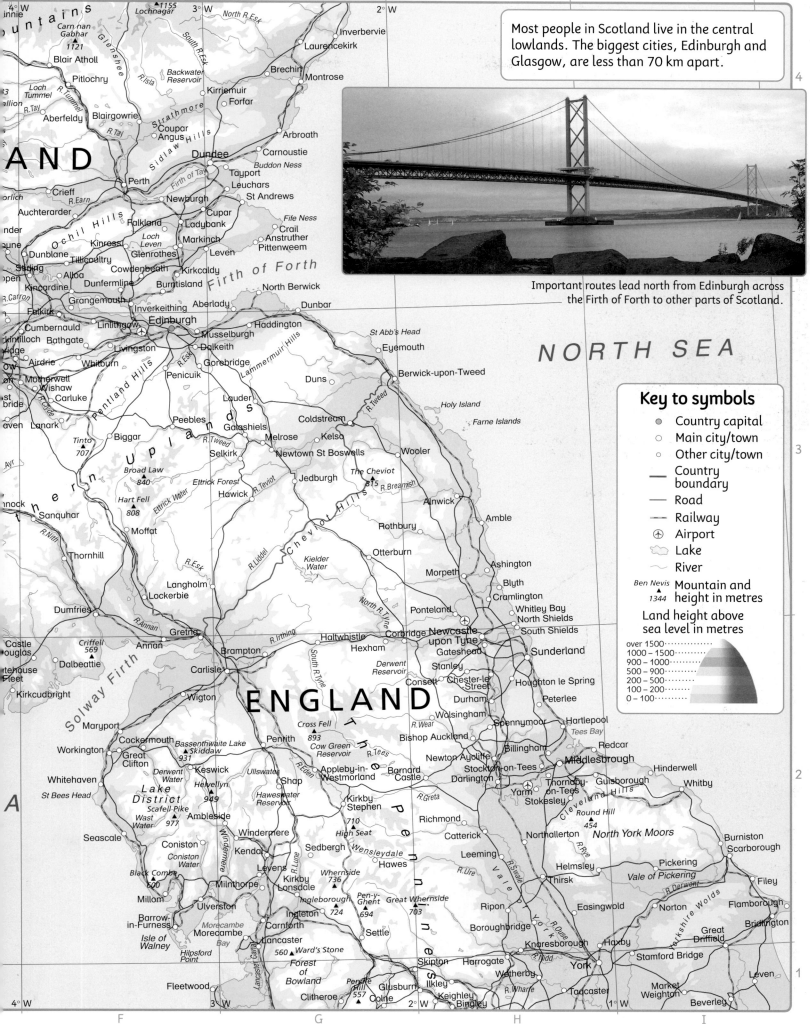

Most people in Scotland live in the central lowlands. The biggest cities, Edinburgh and Glasgow, are less than 70 km apart.

Important routes lead north from Edinburgh across the Firth of Forth to other parts of Scotland.

Key to symbols

- Country capital
- Main city/town
- Other city/town
- Country boundary
- Road
- Railway
- Airport
- Lake
- River
- Ben Nevis 1344 ▲ Mountain and height in metres

Land height above sea level in metres

over 1500	
1000 – 1500	
900 – 1000	
500 – 900	
200 – 500	
100 – 200	
0 – 100	

NORTH SEA

ENGLAND

The Pennine hills run southwards from Scotland through northern England. Old industrial cities such as Manchester, Bradford and Sheffield are found on the edge of the Pennines.

Tourists come to Derwent Water and other parts of the Lake District to enjoy the beautiful scenery.

Scale : One centimetre on this map is the same as 12.5 kilometres on the ground.

0   25   50   75 km

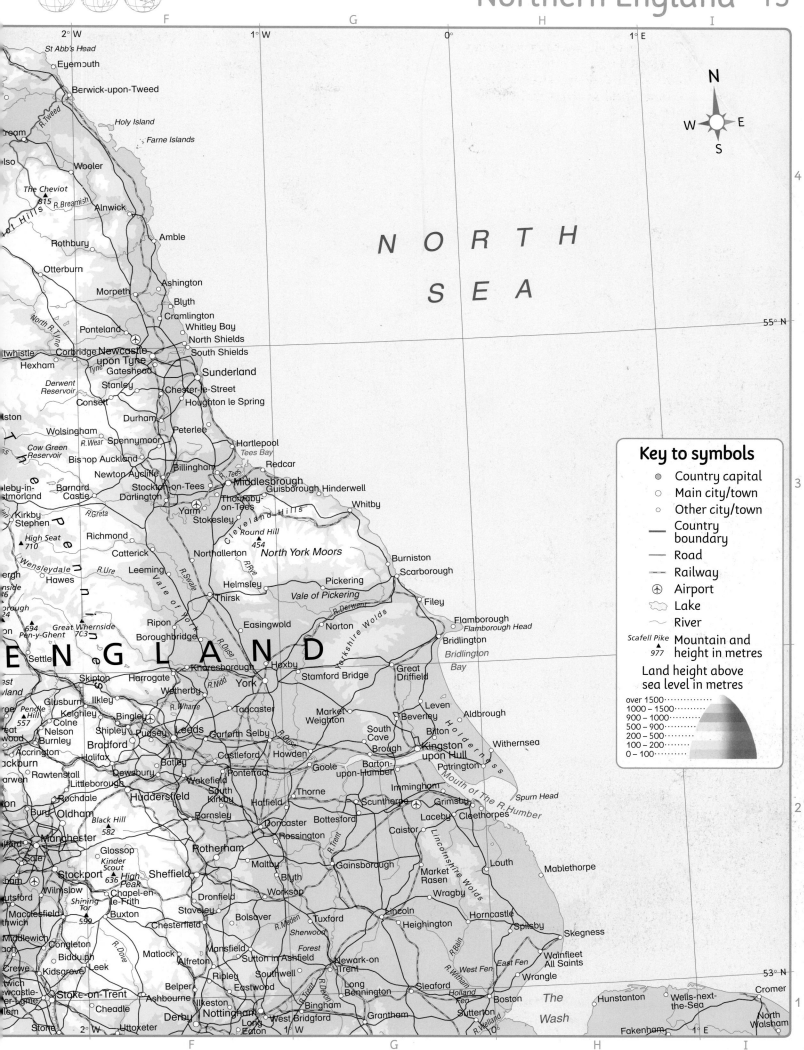

NORTH SEA

ENGLAND

Key to symbols

- ● Country capital
- ○ Main city/town
- ○ Other city/town
- ── Country boundary
- ── Road
- ── Railway
- ✈ Airport
- Lake
- River
- ▲ *Scafell Pike* **Mountain and height in metres**
  977

Land height above sea level in metres

- over 1500
- 1000 – 1500
- 900 – 1000
- 500 – 900
- 200 – 500
- 100 – 200
- 0 – 100

N W E S

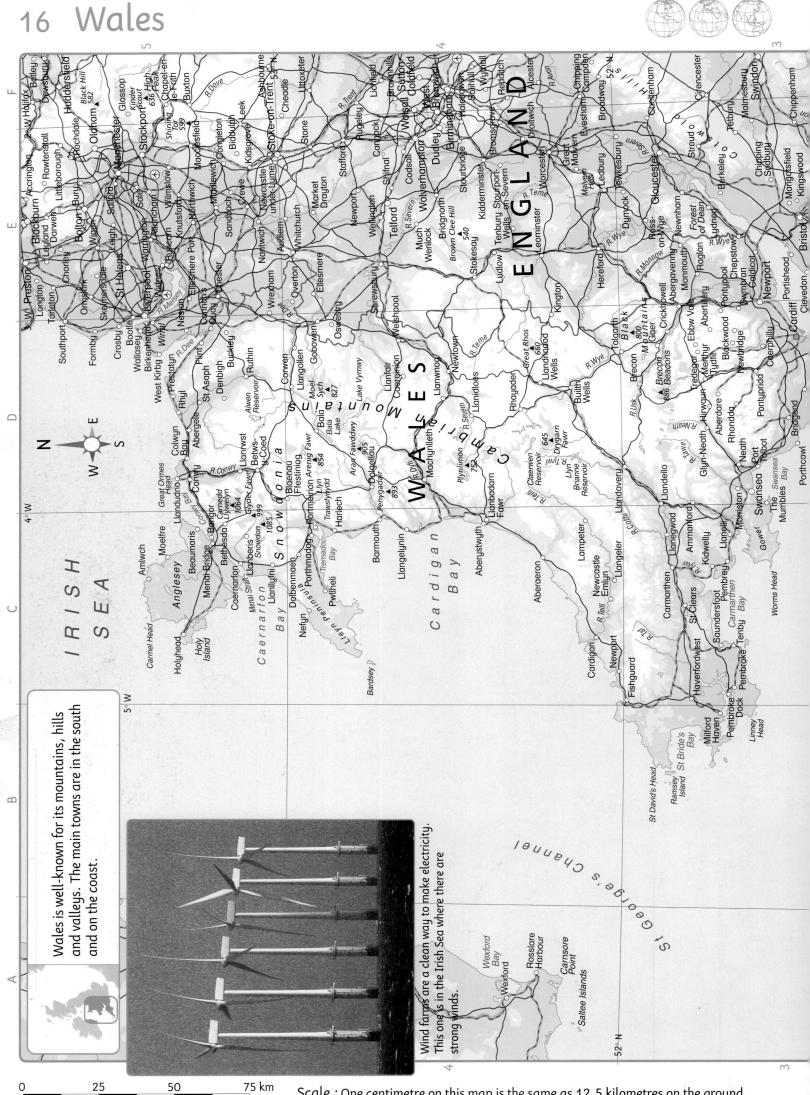

Scale : One centimetre on this map is the same as 12.5 kilometres on the ground.

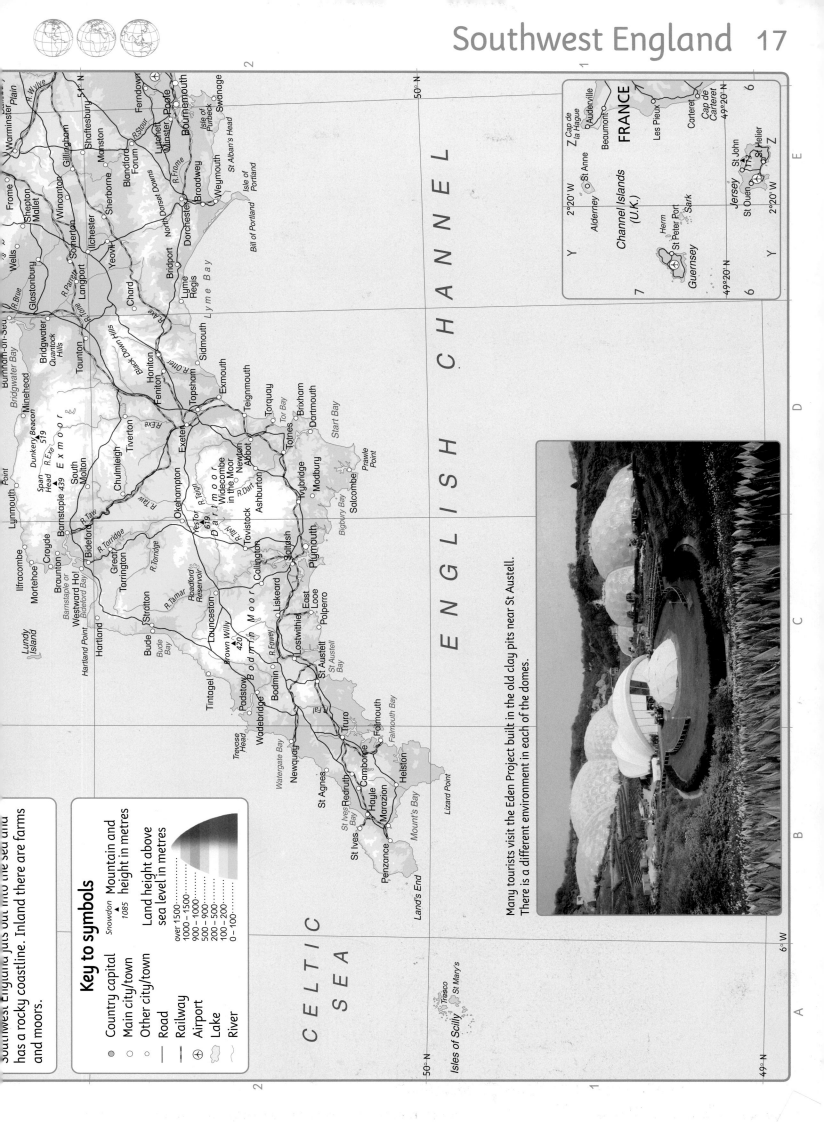

Southwest England juts out into the sea and has a rocky coastline. Inland there are farms and moors.

Key to symbols

- ● Country capital
- ○ Main city/town
- ○ Other city/town
- — Road
- — Railway
- ✈ Airport
- Lake
- River

Snowdon ▲ Mountain and
1085 height in metres

Land height above sea level in metres

| over 1500 |
| 1000–1500 |
| 900–1000 |
| 500–900 |
| 200–500 |
| 100–200 |
| 0–100 |

Many tourists visit the Eden Project built in the old clay pits near St Austell. There is a different environment in each of the domes.

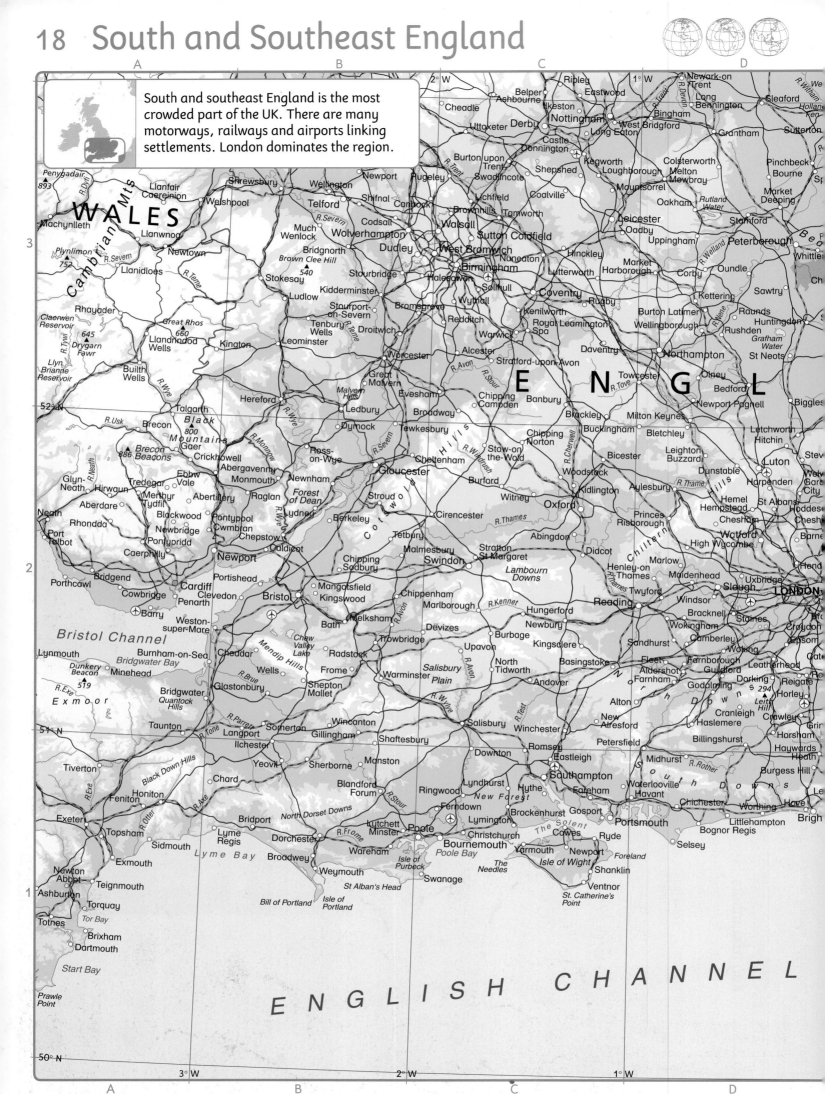

Scale : One centimetre on this map is the same as 12.5 kilometres on the ground.

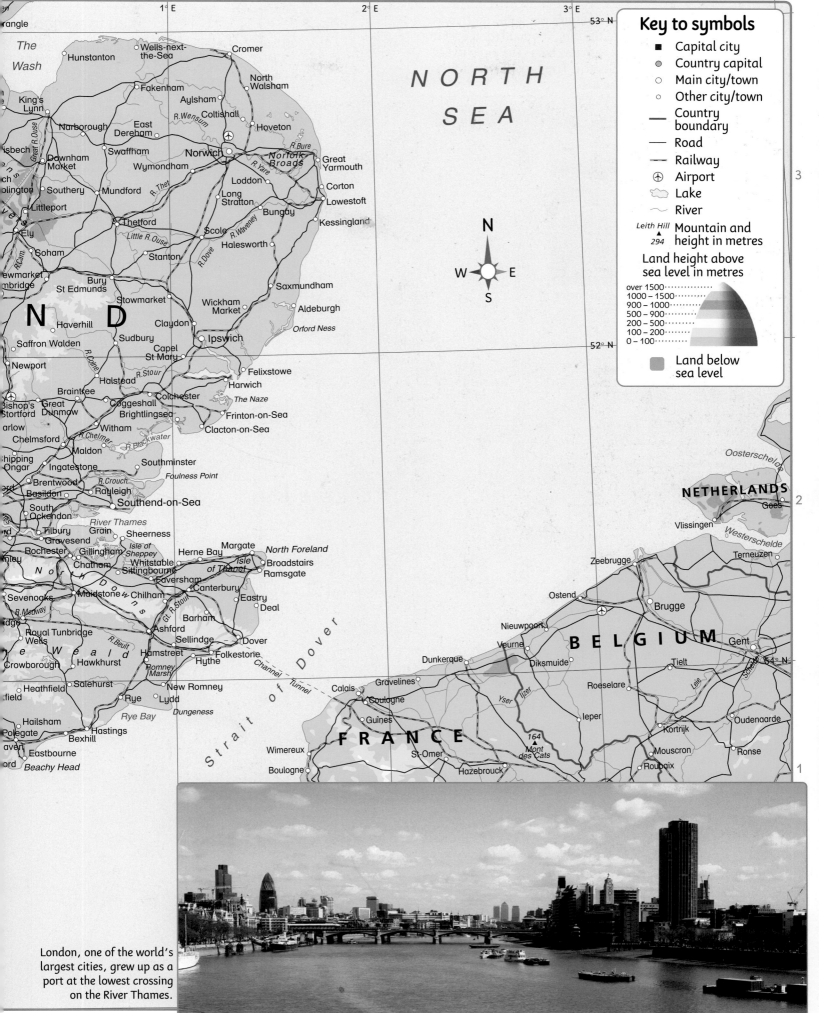

London, one of the world's largest cities, grew up as a port at the lowest crossing on the River Thames.

The highest mountains are in the north and west of Great Britain. The south and east are much flatter with low hills. The main rivers such as the Severn, Trent and Thames flow through these areas.

Key to symbols

Land height above sea level in metres

over 1000
500 – 1000
200 – 500
100 – 200
0 – 100

Ben Nevis
▲
1344 Mountain and height in metres

⌇ River

Lake

Land below sea level

There are mud flats in many river estuaries. These flats are at Applecross in western Scotland.

Total area of the United Kingdom
244 082 sq km

Highest mountain
Ben Nevis 1344 m

ATLANTIC OCEAN

Largest lake
Lough Neagh 396 sq km

North Sea

Largest island
Great Britain 218 476 sq km

Lowest point
The Fens 4 m below sea level

Ireland

Great Britain

Irish Sea

Longest river
River Severn 354 km

Celtic Sea

English Channel

Hound Tor on Dartmoor is made of old, hard rocks.

Channel Islands

Shetland Islands — Mainland — Sumburgh Head

Orkney Islands — Mainland — Hoy — Pentland Firth — Duncansby Head

Cape Wrath

Isle of Lewis — Harris — North Uist — South Uist — Outer Hebrides — The Minch — Skye — Rum — Inner Hebrides — Coll — Tiree — Ben More 966 — Mull — Jura — Islay — Arran

North West Highlands — Moray Firth — R. Spey — Loch Ness — Cairngorm Mts — R. Dee — Ben Macdui 1309 — Ben Nevis ▲ 1344 — Grampian Mts — Glen Coe — R. Tay — Loch Tay — Loch Lomond — Ochil Hills — R. Forth — Firth of Forth — R. Clyde — Firth of Clyde — Southern Uplands — Merrick 843 — R. Tweed — Cheviot Hills — R. Tyne

Malin Head — R. Foyle — R. Bann — Antrim Hills — North Channel — Lough Neagh — Donegal Bay — Lower Lough Erne — Upper Lough Erne — Mourne Mts — Slieve Donard 852 — Dundalk Bay — Achill I. — R. Shannon — Lough Mask — Lough Corrib — Lough Ree — R. Boyne — Galway Bay — Lough Derg — Lugnaquilla Mtn 926 — R. Barrow — Wicklow Mts — R. Shannon — R. Suir — Carrantuohill 1041 — R. Blackwater — St George's Channel — St David's Head

Solway Firth — Scafell Pike 977 — Lake District — Pennines — North York Moors — Flamborough Head — Spurn Head — R. Tees — R. Ouse — High Peak — Kinder Scout 636 — R. Mersey — The Wash — Isle of Man — Anglesey — Snowdon 1085 — R. Dee — Cambrian Mountains — Cardigan Bay — R. Severn — R. Trent — The Fens — Norfolk Broads — R. Avon — R. Great Ouse — Black Mountains 886 — Brecon Beacons — R. Wye — Cotswold Hills — Chiltern Hills — R. Severn — R. Thames — R. Thames — North Downs — South Downs — Beachy Head — Bristol Channel — Exmoor — Mendip Hills — Dartmoor — Yes Tor 619 — R. Tamar — Bodmin Moor — Lyme Bay — Isle of Wight — Start Point — Land's End

0   50   100   150   200   250 km

Scale : One centimetre on this map is the same as 50 kilometres on the ground.

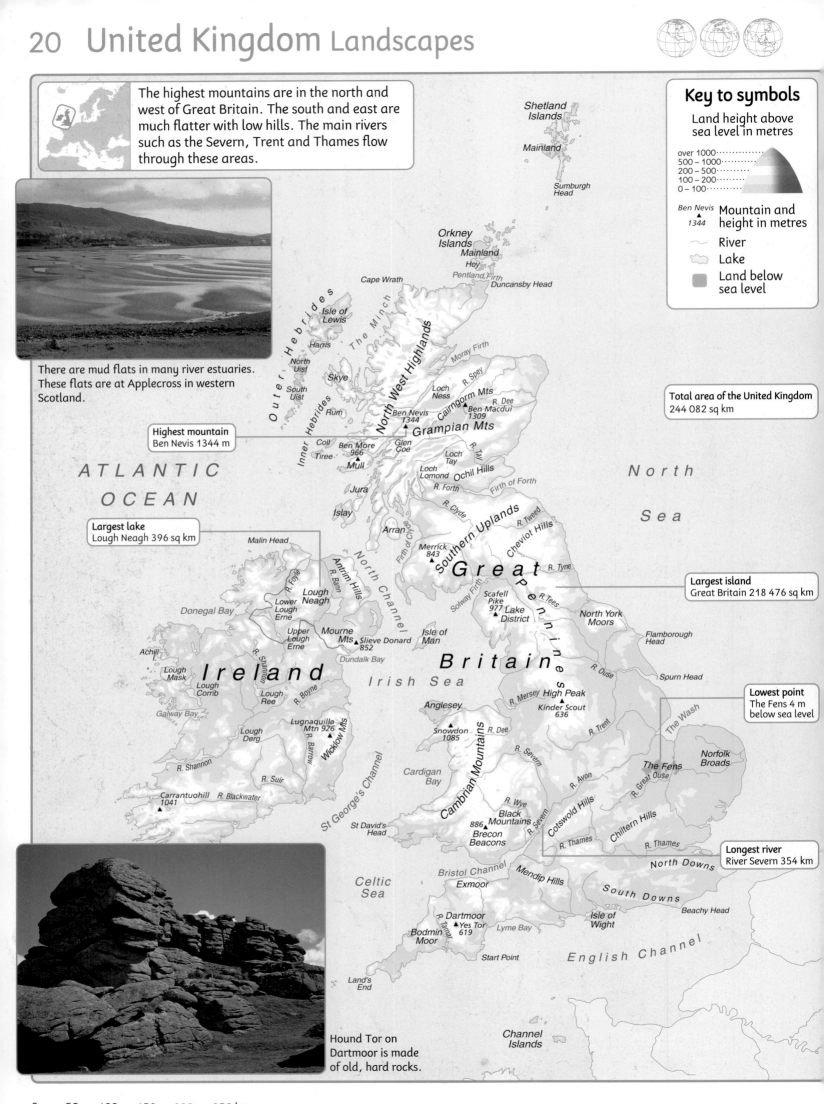

This image was taken from a satellite. It shows the UK and Ireland surrounded by sea. Shallow water is shown in light blue. Cities and built up areas are grey. There is snow in the mountains of Scotland. Can you find where you live?

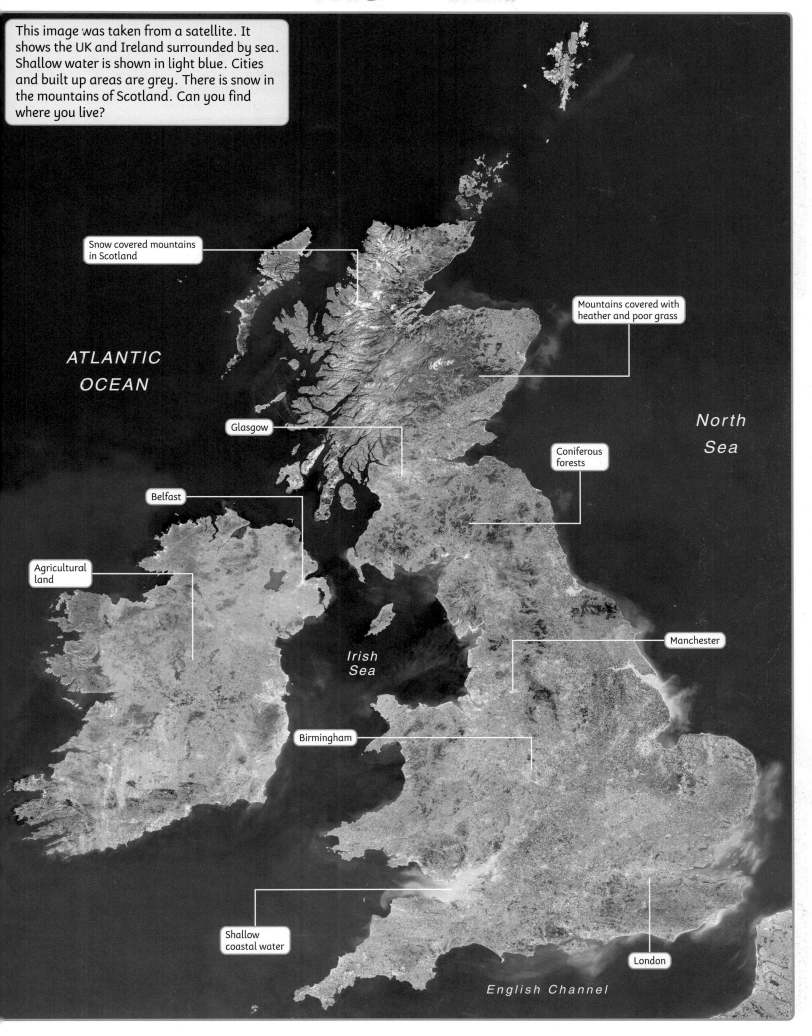

Snow covered mountains in Scotland

Mountains covered with heather and poor grass

ATLANTIC OCEAN

North Sea

Glasgow

Coniferous forests

Belfast

Agricultural land

Manchester

Irish Sea

Birmingham

Shallow coastal water

London

English Channel

The mixture of sun, rain and wind make the weather.

Extreme weather causes problems. In July 2007 torrential rain flooded Tewkesbury and other parts of central England.

Annual rainfall

All parts of the UK have rain throughout the year. Western areas are the wettest. Here winds from the sea shed water as they rise over the mountains.

Average annual rainfall

- more than 2000 mm
- 1500 – 2000 mm
- 1000 – 1500 mm
- 750 – 1000 mm
- 625 – 750 mm
- less than 625 mm
- • Location of places on climate graphs

Braemar

Lowestoft

Southwest winds bring moist air from the Atlantic Ocean

Princetown

Seasonal climate graphs

Braemar
Height 339 metres above sea level

°C / mm
30 / 600
20 / 400
10 / 200
0 / 0

spring summer autumn winter

M A M J J A S O N D J F

Mean monthly temperature

Princetown
Height 453 metres above sea level

°C / mm
30 / 600
20 / 400
10 / 200
0 / 0

spring summer autumn winter

M A M J J A S O N D J F

Lowestoft
Height 25 metres above sea level

°C / mm
30 / 600
20 / 400
10 / 200
0 / 0

spring summer autumn winter

M A M J J A S O N D J F

Average monthly rainfall

Winter temperatures

In January, warm ocean currents bring milder conditions to the southwest of the UK. The coldest areas are the mountains in the north.

Braemar

Lowestoft

Princetown

Average temperature
- over 6°C
- 4 – 6°C
- 2 – 4°C
- 0 – 2°C
- below 0°C
- • Location of places on climate graphs

Summer temperatures

In July, the warmest parts of the UK are in the south, especially along the coasts. Mountain areas are the coolest.

Braemar

Lowestoft

Princetown

Average temperature
- over 16°C
- 14 – 16°C
- 12 – 14°C
- 10 – 12°C
- below 10°C
- • Location of places on climate graphs

Country populations

England 84%

Scotland 8%

Wales 5%

Northern Ireland 3%

More than three quarters of the people in the UK live in England.

Some parts of the UK are much more crowded than others. London and big cities such as Birmingham, Leeds and Glasgow are the most crowded areas. Hill and mountain areas are the emptiest.

UK population change

Population in millions

70
60
50
40
30
20
10
0

1801 1841 1881 1921 1961 2001 2041

Over the last 200 years the number of people living in the UK has increased from 10 to 60 million.

SCOTLAND

Glasgow   Edinburgh

NORTHERN IRELAND   Belfast

IRELAND

Newcastle upon Tyne

Leeds

Liverpool   Manchester

Birmingham

WALES   E N G L A N D

Cardiff   London

Key to symbols

Population per square km

Over 150
10 – 150
0 – 10

Cities and towns in order of size

Where were they born?

Born overseas 8.3%

Born in UK 91.7%

In 2001, over 8% of the UK's population were born overseas. This is more than double the number born overseas in 1951.

50   100   150   200   250 km

Scale : One centimetre on this map is the same as 50 kilometres on the ground.

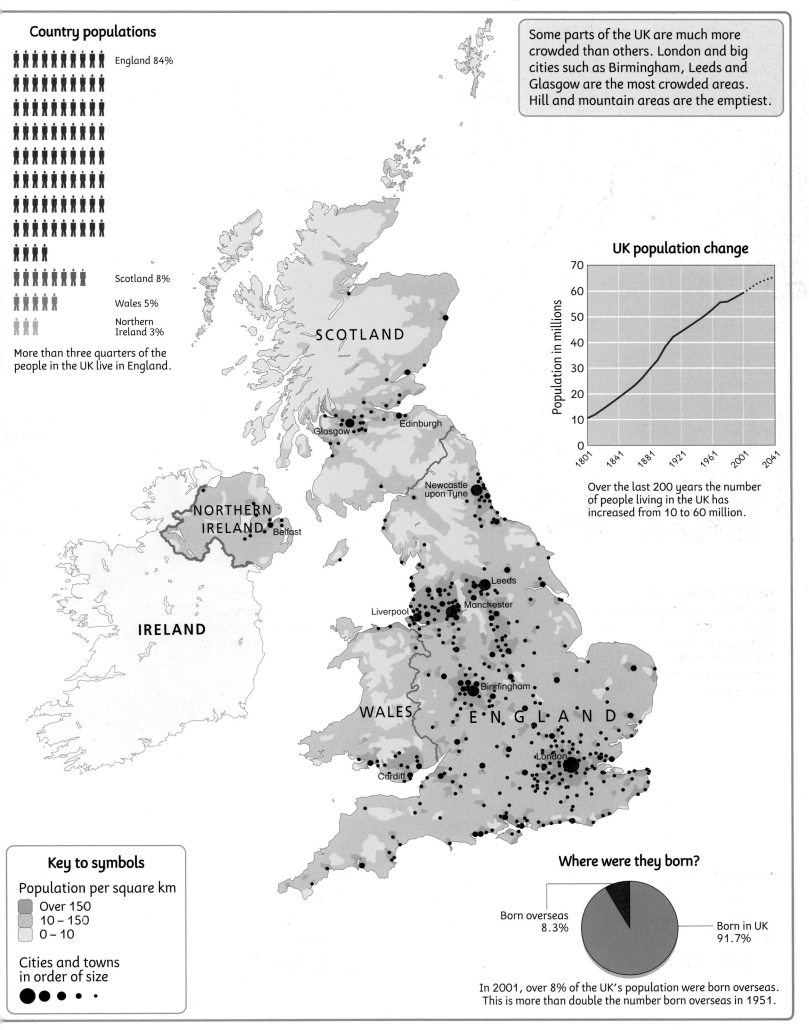

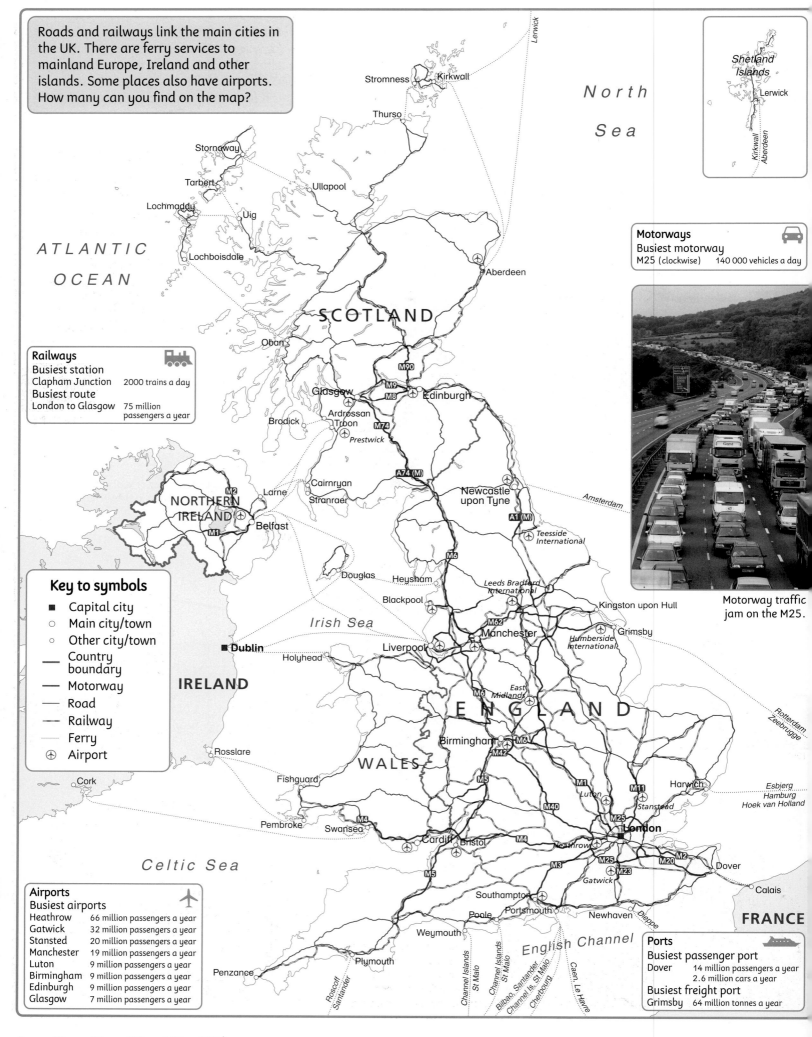

Roads and railways link the main cities in the UK. There are ferry services to mainland Europe, Ireland and other islands. Some places also have airports. How many can you find on the map?

Railways
Busiest station
Clapham Junction 2000 trains a day
Busiest route
London to Glasgow 75 million passengers a year

Key to symbols
- ■ Capital city
- ● Main city/town
- ○ Other city/town
- ── Country boundary
- ── Motorway
- ── Road
- ── Railway
- ···· Ferry
- ⊕ Airport

Motorways
Busiest motorway
M25 (clockwise) 140 000 vehicles a day

Motorway traffic jam on the M25.

Airports
Busiest airports
Heathrow   66 million passengers a year
Gatwick   32 million passengers a year
Stansted   20 million passengers a year
Manchester 19 million passengers a year
Luton   9 million passengers a year
Birmingham 9 million passengers a year
Edinburgh 9 million passengers a year
Glasgow   7 million passengers a year

Ports
Busiest passenger port
Dover   14 million passengers a year
        2.6 million cars a year
Busiest freight port
Grimsby   64 million tonnes a year

North Sea
ATLANTIC OCEAN
Irish Sea
Celtic Sea
English Channel

Shetland Islands
Lerwick
Kirkwall
Aberdeen

SCOTLAND
ENGLAND
WALES
IRELAND
NORTHERN IRELAND
FRANCE

Stromness
Kirkwall
Thurso
Stornoway
Tarbert
Ullapool
Lochmaddy
Uig
Lochboisdale
Oban
Aberdeen
Glasgow
Edinburgh
Brodick
Ardrossan
Troon
Prestwick
Cairnryan
Stranraer
Larne
Belfast
Dublin
Newcastle upon Tyne
Teesside International
Douglas
Heysham
Leeds Bradford International
Blackpool
Kingston upon Hull
Manchester
Grimsby
Liverpool
Humberside International
Holyhead
Rosslare
Cork
Fishguard
East Midlands
Birmingham
Pembroke
Swansea
Cardiff
Bristol
Harwich
Luton
Stanstead
London
Heathrow
Gatwick
Dover
Calais
Southampton
Portsmouth
Poole
Newhaven
Dieppe
Weymouth
Plymouth
Penzance

Amsterdam
Rotterdam Zeebrugge
Esbjerg Hamburg Hoek van Holland

Roscoff Santander
Channel Islands St Malo
Bilbao, Santander Channel Is. St Malo
Caen, Le Havre
Cherbourg

M90
M9
M8
M74
A74 (M)
A1 (M)
M6
M62
M6
M5
M42
M6
M40
M1
M11
M25
M5
M4
M4
M3
M23
M25
M20
M2
M1
M2

Lerwick

Scale : One centimetre on this map is the same as 40 kilometres on the ground.

0   40   80   120   160   200 km

The European Union (EU) was set up in 1957 to keep peace between nations and improve people's lives. Since then it has grown larger and more powerful. It now has 27 member states with others waiting to join.

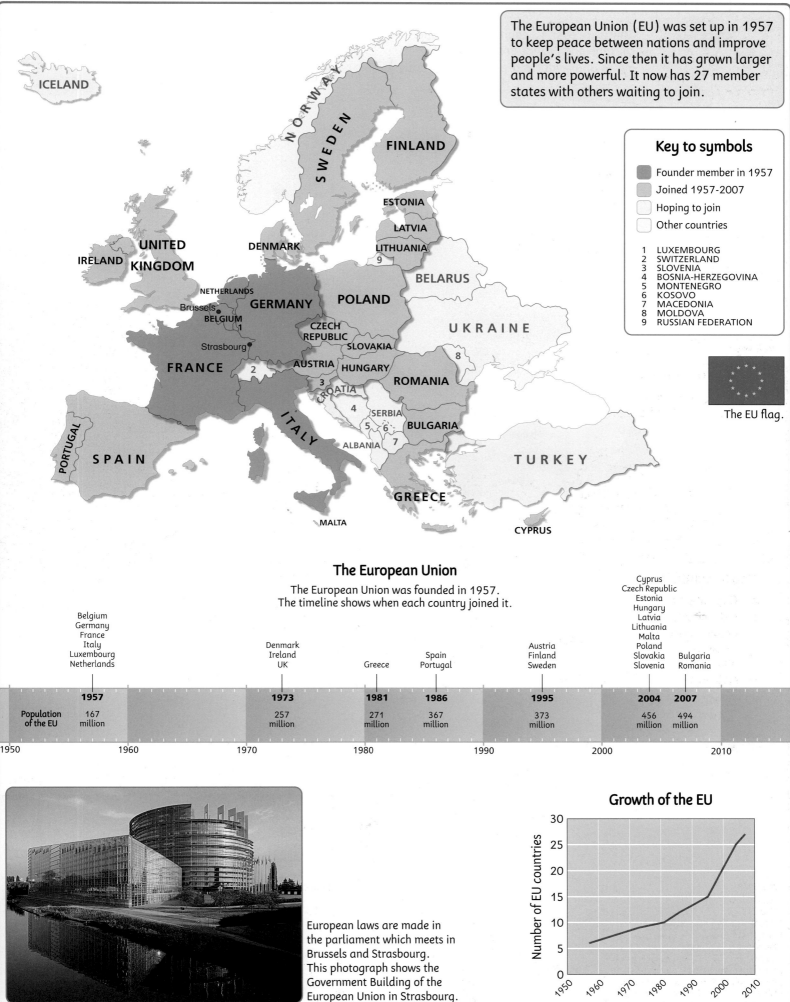

Key to symbols

- Founder member in 1957
- Joined 1957-2007
- Hoping to join
- Other countries

1 LUXEMBOURG
2 SWITZERLAND
3 SLOVENIA
4 BOSNIA-HERZEGOVINA
5 MONTENEGRO
6 KOSOVO
7 MACEDONIA
8 MOLDOVA
9 RUSSIAN FEDERATION

The EU flag.

The European Union

The European Union was founded in 1957.
The timeline shows when each country joined it.

	1957	**1973**	**1981**	**1986**	**1995**	**2004**	**2007**
	Belgium Germany France Italy Luxembourg Netherlands	Denmark Ireland UK	Greece	Spain Portugal	Austria Finland Sweden	Cyprus Czech Republic Estonia Hungary Latvia Lithuania Malta Poland Slovakia Slovenia	Bulgaria Romania
Population of the EU	167 million	257 million	271 million	367 million	373 million	456 million	494 million

1950   1960   1970   1980   1990   2000   2010

European laws are made in the parliament which meets in Brussels and Strasbourg. This photograph shows the Government Building of the European Union in Strasbourg.

Growth of the EU

Number of EU countries

1950 1960 1970 1980 1990 2000 2010

There are over 40 countries in Europe.
Ukraine and France are the largest.
Malta and Andorra are two of the smallest.

ARCTIC OCEAN

Total population of Europe
(excluding Russian Federation)
591 million

Russian Federation
Area 17 million sq km
Population 141 million

Novaya Zemlya

Jan Mayen (Norway)

Country with most people
(excluding Russian Federation)
Germany 82 million

ICELAND
Reykjavík

ATLANTIC OCEAN

White Sea

Faroe Islands (Denmark)

RUSSIAN FEDERATION

NORWAY
SWEDEN
FINLAND

Oslo
Stockholm
Helsinki
St Petersburg
Tallinn
ESTONIA
LATVIA
Riga
LITHUANIA
Vilnius
Minsk

Moscow

Largest country
(excluding Russian Federation)
Ukraine 603 700 sq km

Edinburgh *North Sea*
Belfast
Dublin
IRELAND
UNITED KINGDOM
DENMARK
Copenhagen
Baltic Sea
10

Berlin
GERMANY
POLAND
Warsaw
BELARUS

London
Prague
CZECH REPUBLIC
SLOVAKIA
Kiev
UKRAINE
Volgograd

English Channel
Paris
1
2
3
Munich
Vienna
Bratislava
AUSTRIA
HUNGARY
Budapest
MOLDOVA
Chişinău
Odesa

Largest city
(Western Europe)
Paris 10 million

FRANCE
Lyon
4
5
Milan
Zagreb
CROATIA
Belgrade
ROMANIA
Bucharest
Caspian Sea

Bay of Biscay
SAN MARINO
6
SERBIA
Black Sea

PORTUGAL
ANDORRA
Corsica
Rome
ITALY
Adriatic Sea
7 8
Skopje
9
BULGARIA
Sofia
Istanbul

Largest city
Istanbul 11 million

Lisbon
Madrid
SPAIN
Barcelona
Balearic Islands
Tirana
ALBANIA
TURKEY

Sardinia
GREECE
Aegean Sea
ASIA

Palma de Mallorca

Strait of Gibraltar
Gibraltar (UK)
Mediterranean Sea
Sicily
Athens
Crete
Rhodes

MALTA

1 NETHERLANDS
2 BELGIUM
3 LUXEMBOURG
4 SWITZERLAND
5 SLOVENIA
6 BOSNIA-HERZEGOVINA
7 MONTENEGRO
8 KOSOVO
9 MACEDONIA
10 RUSSIAN FEDERATION

AFRICA

Key to symbols

◩ Countries
■ Capital city
○ Important city/town

Ancient buildings around
Red Square, Moscow.

0 250 500 750 1000 1250 1500 km

Scale : One centimetre on this map is the same as 250 kilometres on the ground.

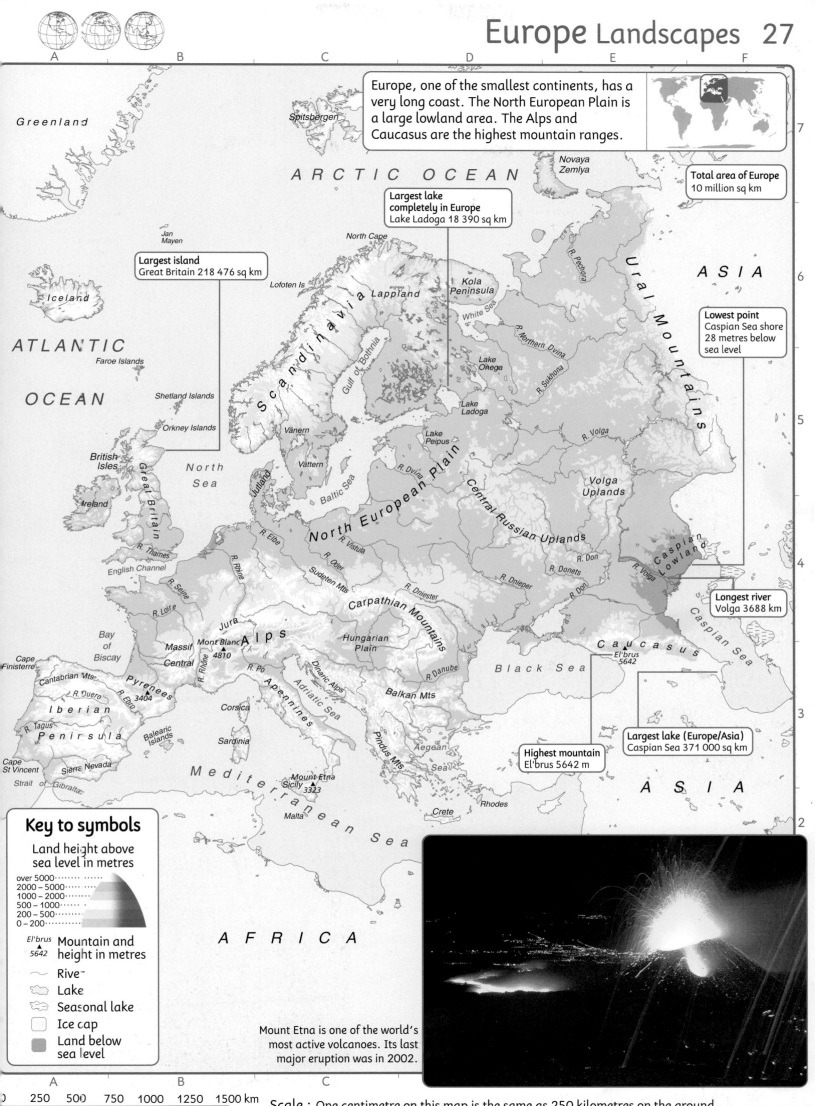

A B C D E F

Greenland

Spitsbergen

ARCTIC OCEAN

Novaya Zemlya

Europe, one of the smallest continents, has a very long coast. The North European Plain is a large lowland area. The Alps and Caucasus are the highest mountain ranges.

Total area of Europe
10 million sq km

Largest lake completely in Europe
Lake Ladoga 18 390 sq km

Jan Mayen

North Cape

ASIA

Iceland

Largest island
Great Britain 218 476 sq km

Lofoten Is

Kola Peninsula

White Sea

Lowest point
Caspian Sea shore 28 metres below sea level

ATLANTIC

Faroe Islands

Scandinavia

Lappland

R. Pechora

Ural Mountains

OCEAN

Shetland Islands

Orkney Islands

Lake Onega

R. Northern Dvina

R. Sukhona

British Isles

North Sea

Vänern

Gulf of Bothnia

Lake Ladoga

R. Volga

Ireland

Vättern

Lake Peipus

Volga Uplands

Great Britain

Baltic Sea

R. Dvina

Central Russian Uplands

Caspian Lowland

R. Thames

Jutland

R. Elbe

North European Plain

R. Vistula

R. Oder

R. Don

R. Donets

R. Volga

Caspian Sea

English Channel

R. Seine

R. Rhine

Sudeten Mts

R. Dniester

R. Dnieper

R. Don

Longest river
Volga 3688 km

R. Loire

Carpathian Mountains

Bay of Biscay

Jura

Massif Central

Alps

Mont Blanc ▲ 4810

Hungarian Plain

R. Rhône

R. Danube

Black Sea

Caucasus

El'brus 5642

Largest lake (Europe/Asia)
Caspian Sea 371 000 sq km

Cape Finisterre

Cantabrian Mts

Pyrenees ▲ 3404

R. Po

Dinaric Alps

Adriatic Sea

Apennines

Balkan Mts

R. Duero

R. Ebro

Corsica

Iberian Peninsula

R. Tagus

Sierra Nevada

Balearic Islands

Sardinia

Pindus Mts

Aegean Sea

Highest mountain
El'brus 5642 m

Cape St Vincent

Strait of Gibraltar

Mediterranean Sea

Mount Etna Sicily ▲ 3323

Malta

Crete

Rhodes

ASIA

AFRICA

Key to symbols

Land height above sea level in metres

- over 5000
- 2000 – 5000
- 1000 – 2000
- 500 – 1000
- 200 – 500
- 0 – 200

El'brus ▲ 5642 Mountain and height in metres

~ River

Lake

Seasonal lake

Ice cap

Land below sea level

Mount Etna is one of the world's most active volcanoes. Its last major eruption was in 2002.

A B C

0 250 500 750 1000 1250 1500 km

Scale : One centimetre on this map is the same as 250 kilometres on the ground.

Three Scandinavian countries – Norway, Sweden and Denmark – lie at the heart of northern Europe. They have similar traditions and beliefs. In the past, the people who lived there also all spoke the same language.

Scale : One centimetre on this map is the same as 100 kilometres on the ground

0 100 200 300 400 500 600 700 800 km

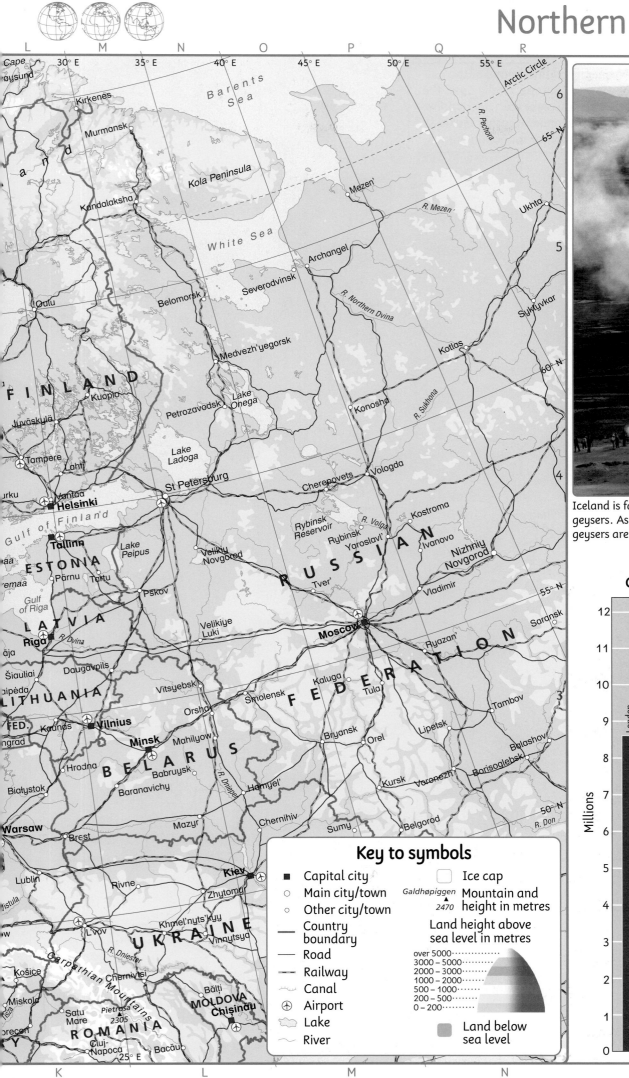

Iceland is famous for hot springs and geysers. As well as attracting tourists, geysers are a valuable source of power.

Capital populations

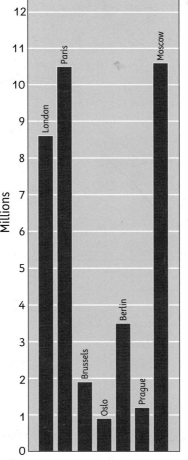

Key to symbols

- ■ Capital city
- ○ Main city/town
- ○ Other city/town
- —— Country boundary
- —— Road
- —— Railway
- ⊣⊢ Canal
- ✈ Airport
- Lake
- River

- ☐ Ice cap
- *Galdhøpiggen* ▲ Mountain and
- *2470* height in metres
- Land height above sea level in metres
  - over 5000
  - 3000 – 5000
  - 2000 – 3000
  - 1000 – 2000
  - 500 – 1000
  - 200 – 500
  - 0 – 200
- Land below sea level

The Mediterranean Sea links many of the countries of southern Europe. In the past, the Romans and Ancient Greeks both had empires here. Today, good summer weather makes the Mediterranean popular for holidays.

ATLANTIC OCEAN

UNITED KINGDOM
Birmingham
Oxford
Bristol
London
Southampton
Dover
Strait of Dover
English Channel
Channel Islands
Brest
Le Havre
Caen
Rennes
Le Mans
Nantes
R. Loire
Bay of Biscay
La Rochelle
Poitiers
R. Loire
Tours
Orléans
Paris
Norwich
Amiens
Rouen
R. Seine
Lille
Calais
BELGIUM
Brussels
Brugge
Antwerp
Liège
Eindhoven
Duisburg
Dijon
R. Seine
Reims
Nancy
Strasbourg
LUXEMBOURG
Luxembourg
Mainz
Frankfurt

NETHERLANDS
Amsterdam
The Hague
Rotterdam
Groningen
IJsselmeer
R. Wesel

GERMANY
Bremen
Bielefeld
Hannover
Dortmund
Essen
Düsseldorf
Cologne
Bonn
R. Rhine
Leipzig
Erfurt
Magde
Ber
Dres
Karlsruhe
Stuttgart
Nuremberg
Munich
Sal

FRANCE
A Coruña
Cape Finisterre
Vigo
Braga
Oporto
Coimbra
Lisbon
PORTUGAL
Gijón
Santander
Cantabrian Mountains
León
R. Douro
R. Duero
Bilbao
Burgos
Valladolid
Salamanca
Madrid
R. Tagus
Badajoz
SPAIN
Bayonne
Bordeaux
R. Garonne
Toulouse
Limoges
Clermont-Ferrand
Massif Central
Montpellier
Lyon
Grenoble
R. Rhône
Mont Blanc 4810
Avignon
Marseille
Perpignan
Côte d'Azur
Nice
Monte Carlo
MONACO

Pamplona
Zaragoza
R. Ebro
Pyrenees
Aneto 3404
ANDORRA
Andorra la Vella
Barcelona
Costa Brava
Valencia
Albacete

SWITZERLAND
Basel
Geneva
Bern
Zürich
Innsbruck
LIECHTENSTEIN
Milan
Turin
Verona
Piacenza
Genoa
Bologna
R. Po
Veni
Bolzano
SAN MARINO
Sa
Ma
Florence
Pisa
Perugia
A
ITALY
Ar
Rome

Sierra Morena
Córdoba
R. Guadalquivir
Seville
Faro
Cádiz
Cape St Vincent
Granada
Sierra Nevada
Málaga
Costa del Sol
Almería
Gibraltar (UK)
Strait of Gibraltar
Ceuta (Spain)
Tangier
Tétouan
Melilla (Spain)
Alicante
Cartagena
Palma de Mallorca
Ibiza
Majorca
Minorca
Balearic Islands
Mediterranean Sea
Corsica
Ajaccio
Sardinia
Sassari
Cagliari
Tyrrhenian Sea
Palermo

MOROCCO
Rabat
Casablanca
Fez
Meknès
Oujda
Marrakesh
Beni Mellal
Oran
Sidi Bel Abbès
Ech Chélif
Sétif
Algiers
Constantine
ALGERIA
Batna
Tébessa
Saharan Atlas
Annaba
Bizerte
Tunis
TUNISIA
Sousse
Sfax
Gafsa
Gulf of Gabès

15° W   10° W   5° W   0°   5° E   10° E
45° N
40° N
35° N

Cross section through the Alps

Height in metres

France   Swiss Alps   Italy   Austrian Alps
Montpellier   Grenoble   Mont Blanc   Bolzano   Graz
River Rhône

5000
4000
3000
2000
1000
0

Height in metre
5000
4000
3000
2000
1000
0

0   100   200   300   400   500   600   700   800 km

Scale : One centimetre on this map is the same as 100 kilometres on the ground.

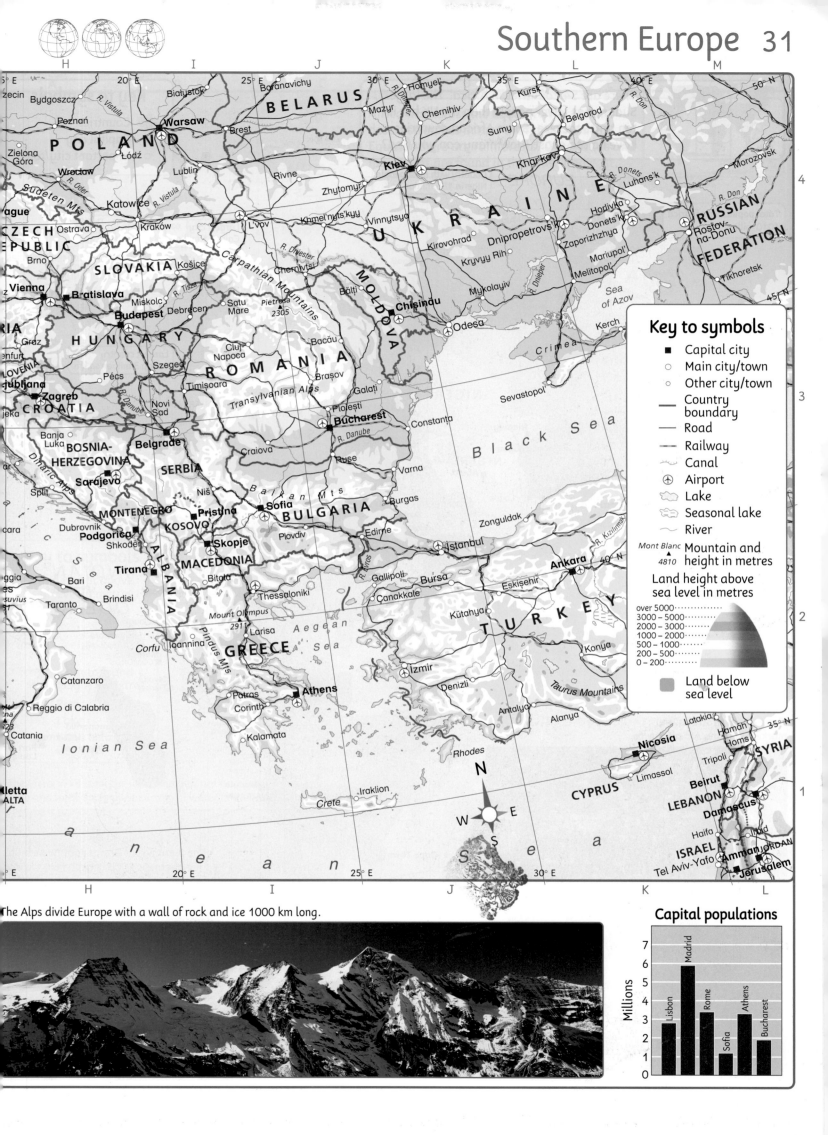

Key to symbols
- ■ Capital city
- ○ Main city/town
- ○ Other city/town
- — Country boundary
- — Road
- —|— Railway
- Canal
- ⊕ Airport
- Lake
- Seasonal lake
- River
- Mont Blanc ▲ Mountain and
- 4810 height in metres

Land height above sea level in metres
- over 5000
- 3000 – 5000
- 1000 – 2000
- 500 – 1000
- 200 – 500
- 0 – 200

Land below sea level

The Alps divide Europe with a wall of rock and ice 1000 km long.

Capital populations

Millions
7
6
5
4
3
2
1
0

Lisbon, Madrid, Rome, Sofia, Athens, Bucharest

Canada, Mexico and the USA make up most of North America. Many small countries are found in the narrow belt of land which leads to South America and in the Caribbean Sea.

ARCTIC OCEAN

GREENLAND (Denmark)

Baffin Bay

Total population of North America 539 million

ALASKA U.S.A.

Anchorage

Nuuk (Godthåb)

Iqaluit

Largest country Canada 10 million sq km

Great Bear Lake

Great Slave Lake

Hudson Bay

St John's

C A N A D A

Edmonton

Calgary

Vancouver

Quebec

Halifax

PACIFIC OCEAN

Seattle

Winnipeg

Montreal

Portland

Lake Superior

Lake Huron

Ottawa

Toronto

Lake Ontario

Boston

ATLANTIC OCEAN

Minneapolis

Lake Michigan

Detroit

Lake Erie

New York

Sacramento

U N I T E D   S T A T E S

Chicago

Pittsburgh

Washington D.C.

San Francisco

Salt Lake City

Denver

Kansas City

St Louis

O F   A M E R I C A

Bermuda (UK)

Los Angeles

San Diego

Phoenix

Dallas

Atlanta

Country with most people USA 315 million

El Paso

Houston

New Orleans

Miami

THE BAHAMAS

ANTIGUA AND BARBUDA

Nassau

Monterrey

Gulf of Mexico

Havana

DOMINICAN REPUBLIC

CUBA

HAITI

PUERTO RICO (USA)

DOMINICA

ST LUCIA

BARBAD

MEXICO

JAMAICA

Kingston

Caribbean Sea

GRENADA

Largest city Mexico City 20 million

Guadalajara

Mexico City

Puebla

BELIZE

HONDURAS

Manhattan in the centre of New York is a centre for business and entertainment.

GUATEMALA

Guatemala City

NICARAGUA

EL SALVADOR

Managua

Panama City

COSTA RICA

PANAMA

SOUTH

AMERICA

Key to symbols

Countries

■ Capital city

○ Important city/town

Scale : One centimetre on this map is the same as 400 kilometres on the ground

0   400   800   1200   1600   2000   2400   2800   3200 km

The Rocky Mountains stretch down the western side of North America. Further east there are lakes and plains. In the north, Greenland is covered in ice.

ARCTIC OCEAN

Greenland

Baffin Bay

Ellesmere Island

Davis Strait

Total area of North America
25 million sq km

Largest island
Greenland 2 million sq km

Cape Farewell

Baffin Island

Victoria Island

R. Yukon

▲ Mount McKinley
6194

Largest lake
Lake Superior 82 100 sq km

Great Bear Lake

▲ Mount Logan
5959

Gulf of Alaska

Great Slave Lake

R. Mackenzie

Labrador

Highest mountain
Mount McKinley 6194 m

Coast Mountains

R. Peace

Hudson Bay

Newfoundland

PACIFIC OCEAN

R o *c* k y
3954 ▲

Canadian Shield

R. St. Lawrence

Lowest point
Death Valley
86 metres below
sea level

Great Plains

R. Snake

Lake Superior
Great Lakes
Lake Huron   Lake Ontario   *Cape Cod*
Niagara Falls

ATLANTIC OCEAN

Great Basin

Great Salt Lake

Mount Elbert ▲
4398

R. North Platte

R. Missouri

Lake Michigan

Lake Erie

Key to symbols

Land height above sea level in metres

over 5000
2000 – 5000
1000 – 2000
500 – 1000
200 – 500
0 – 200

Mount McKinley ▲ Mountain and height in metres
6194

⌢ River

Lake

Seasonal lake

Ice cap

Land below sea level

Mount Whitney ▲
4418

Death Valley

Grand Canyon

R. Colorado

R. Red

R. Ohio

R. Mississippi

Appalachian Mountains
▲ 2037

Longest river
Mississippi-Missouri 5969 km

R. Brazos

Rio Grande

Florida

Sierra Madre Occidental

Sierra Madre Oriental

Gulf of California

Gulf of Mexico

Cuba   *Hispaniola*

Popocatépetl ▲
5452

Yucatán

Caribbean Sea

The Grand Canyon on the Colorado River is 1500 metres deep and over 400 km long. It was one of the first National Parks in the USA.

Lake Nicaragua   *Isthmus of Panama*

SOUTH AMERICA

400 800 1200 1600 2000 2400 2800 3200 km

Scale : One centimetre on this map is the same as 400 kilometres on the ground.

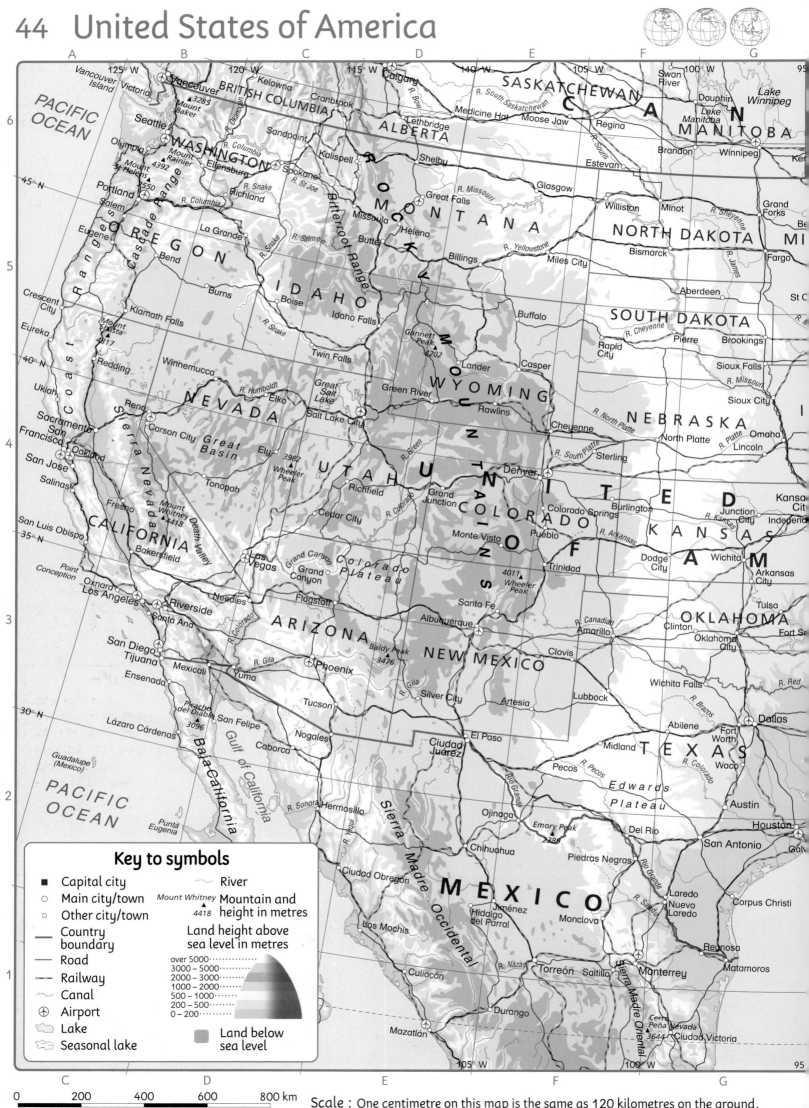

Key to symbols

- ■ Capital city
- ○ Main city/town
- ○ Other city/town
- ▬▬ Country boundary
- ── Road
- ╫── Railway
- ∿ Canal
- ⊕ Airport
- 🗺 Lake
- 🗺 Seasonal lake
- ∿ River
- ▲ *Mount Whitney* 4418 Mountain and height in metres

Land height above sea level in metres

| over 5000 |
| 3000 – 5000 |
| 2000 – 3000 |
| 1000 – 2000 |
| 500 – 1000 |
| 200 – 500 |
| 0 – 200 |

Land below sea level

Scale : One centimetre on this map is the same as 120 kilometres on the ground.

0   200   400   600   800 km

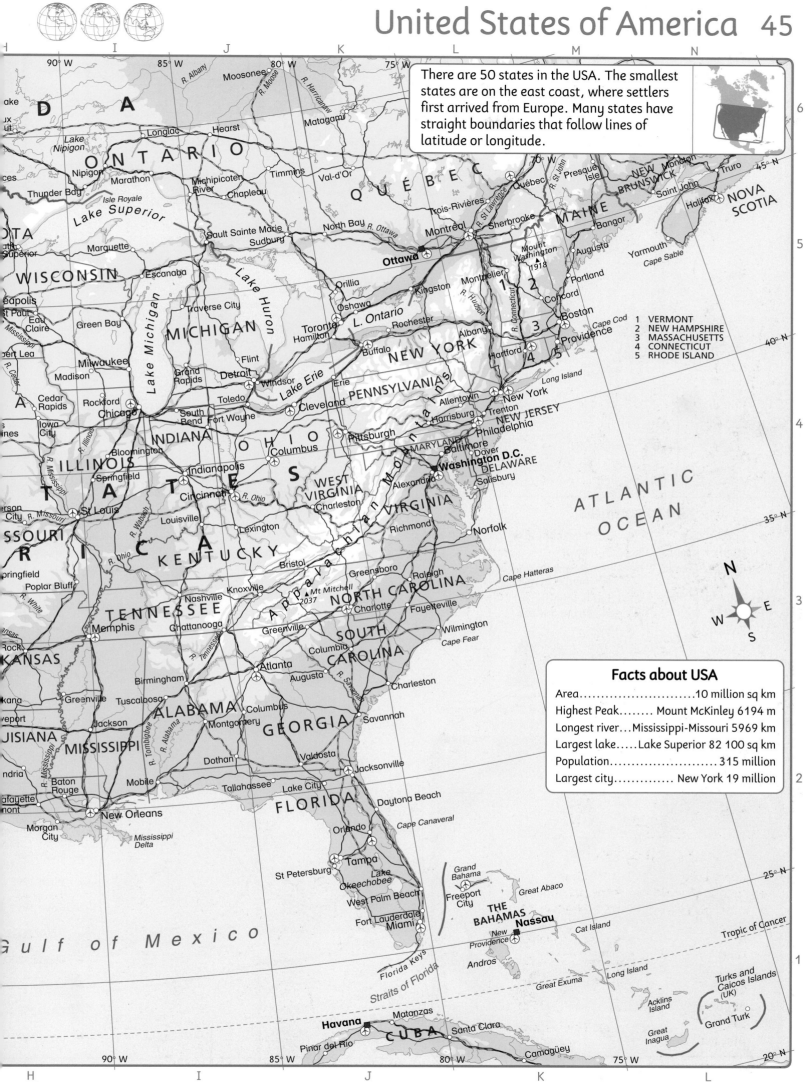

There are 50 states in the USA. The smallest states are on the east coast, where settlers first arrived from Europe. Many states have straight boundaries that follow lines of latitude or longitude.

1 VERMONT
2 NEW HAMPSHIRE
3 MASSACHUSETTS
4 CONNECTICUT
5 RHODE ISLAND

Facts about USA

Area...........................10 million sq km
Highest Peak........ Mount McKinley 6194 m
Longest river...Mississippi-Missouri 5969 km
Largest lake.....Lake Superior 82 100 sq km
Population.........................315 million
Largest city............. New York 19 million

Key to symbols

- ■ Capital city
- ○ Main city/town
- ○ Other city/town
- — Country boundary
- — Road
- — Railway
- ⌇ Canal
- ⊕ Airport
- ⌇ Lake
- ⌇ Seasonal lake
- ~ River
- ▲ *Popocatépetl* Mountain and
  5452 height in metres

Land height above
sea level in metres

over 5000	
3000 – 5000	
2000 – 3000	
1000 – 2000	
500 – 1000	
200 – 500	
0 – 200	

Hurricane Katrina destroyed New Orleans in August 2005. The centre of the storm shows up clearly in this photograph from the air.

Tracks of major hurricanes

- → Gordon 1994
- → Fran 1996
- → Mitch 1998
- → Floyd 1999
- → Isabel 2003
- → Charley 200
- → Katrina 2005
- → Rita 2005
- → Dean 2007

Scale : One centimetre on this map is the same as 135 kilometres on the ground.

0   200   400   600   800 km

Mexico is eight times the size of the UK. With many high mountains, it has a population of over 100 million people. The Caribbean Sea to the east is dotted with islands. These are popular with tourists.

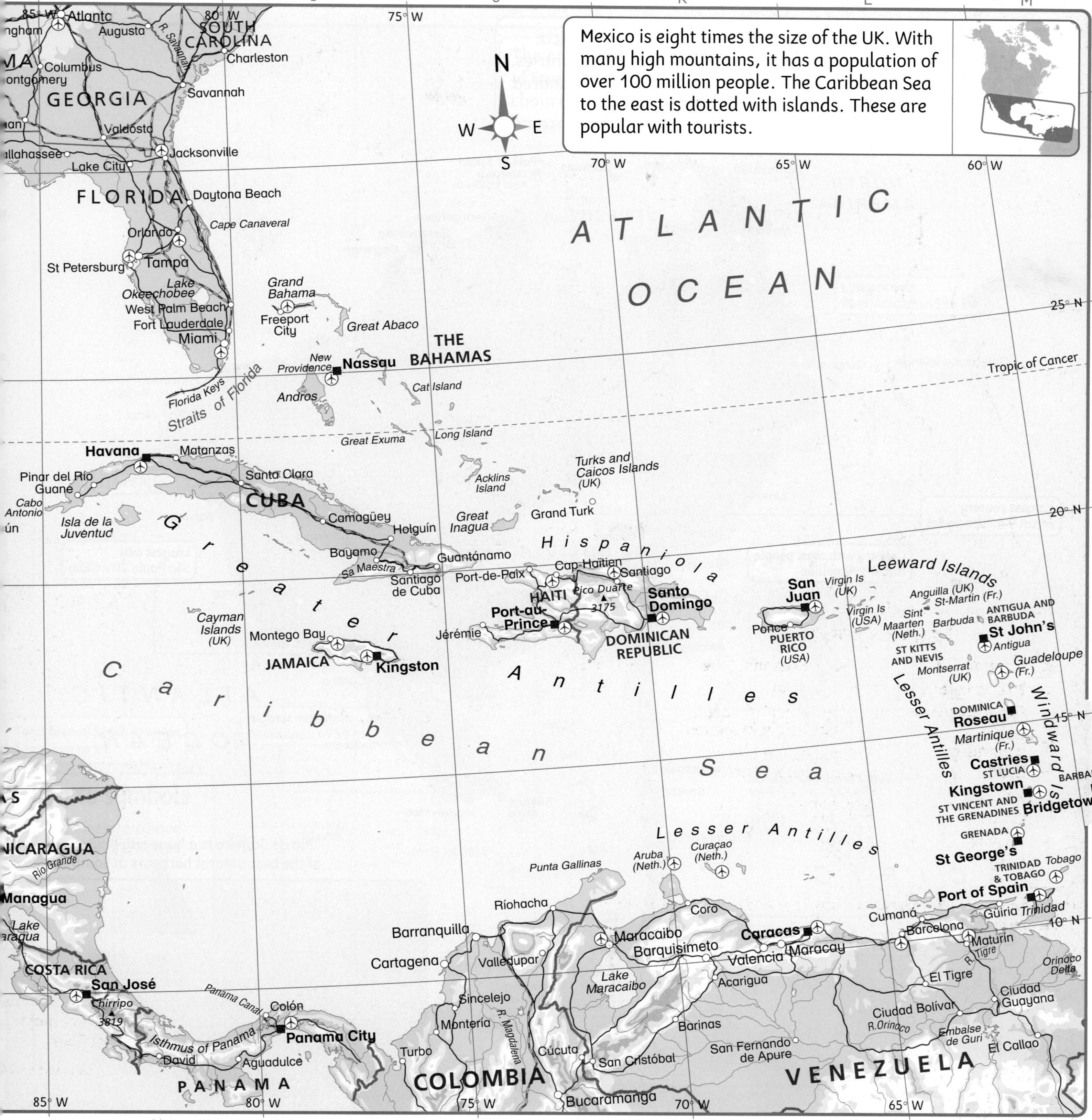

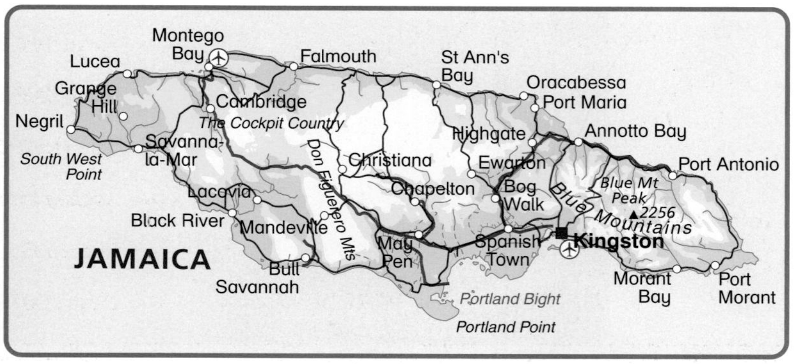

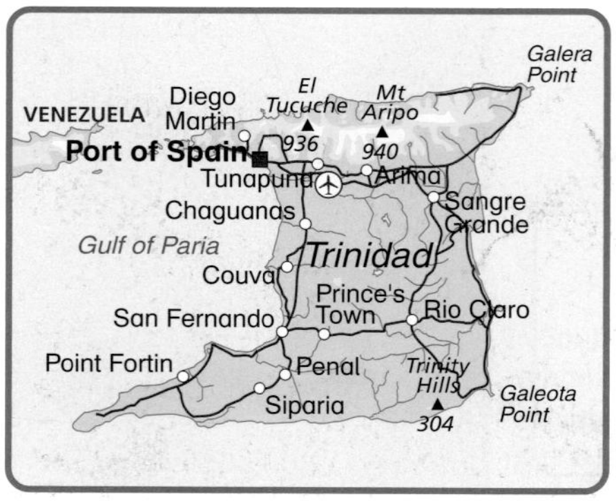

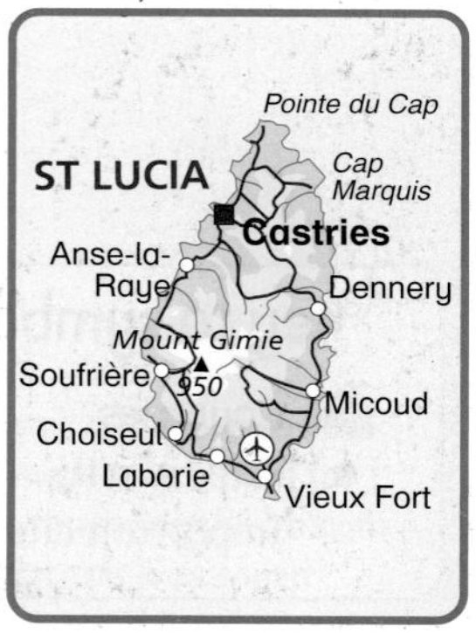

Map grid references (top): H, I, J, K, L, M
Latitude/Longitude labels: 85° W, 80° W, 75° W, 70° W, 65° W, 60° W

25° N
Tropic of Cancer
20° N
15° N
10° N

Main map labels

Atlanta
Augusta
Columbus
Montgomery
GEORGIA
Valdosta
Tallahassee
Lake City
Jacksonville
SOUTH CAROLINA
Charleston
Savannah
R. Savannah

FLORIDA
Daytona Beach
Orlando
Cape Canaveral
St Petersburg
Tampa
Lake Okeechobee
West Palm Beach
Fort Lauderdale
Miami
Florida Keys
Straits of Florida

N
W E
S

ATLANTIC OCEAN

Grand Bahama
Freeport City
Great Abaco
THE BAHAMAS
New Providence
Nassau
Cat Island
Andros
Great Exuma
Long Island
Acklins Island
Turks and Caicos Islands (UK)
Great Inagua
Grand Turk

Havana
Matanzas
Pinar del Río
Guane
Cabo Antonio
ún
Isla de la Juventud
CUBA
Santa Clara
Camagüey
Holguín
Bayamo
Sa Maestra
Guantánamo
Santiago de Cuba
Port-de-Paix
Cap-Haïtien
Santiago
Hispaniola
HAITI
Pico Duarte 3175
Port-au-Prince
Jérémie
DOMINICAN REPUBLIC
Santo Domingo
Greater Antilles

Cayman Islands (UK)
Montego Bay
JAMAICA
Kingston

San Juan
Virgin Is (UK)
Virgin Is (USA)
Ponce
PUERTO RICO (USA)
Leeward Islands
Anguilla (UK)
St-Martin (Fr.)
Sint Maarten (Neth.)
Barbuda
ANTIGUA AND BARBUDA
St John's
Antigua
ST KITTS AND NEVIS
Montserrat (UK)
Guadeloupe (Fr.)
DOMINICA
Roseau
Martinique (Fr.)
Lesser Antilles
Castries ST LUCIA
BARBADOS
Kingstown
ST VINCENT AND THE GRENADINES
Bridgetown
GRENADA
St George's
Windward Is
TRINIDAD & TOBAGO
Tobago
Port of Spain
Güiria Trinidad
Cumaná
Barcelona
Maturín

Caribbean Sea
Lesser Antilles

NICARAGUA
Rio Grande
Managua
Lake Nicaragua
COSTA RICA
San José
Chirripó 3819
Panama Canal
Colón
Isthmus of Panama
David
Aguadulce
Panama City
PANAMA
Turbo
Barranquilla
Cartagena
Sincelejo
Montería
R. Magdalena
COLOMBIA
Bucaramanga
San Cristóbal
Cúcuta
Punta Gallinas
Ríohacha
Valledupar
Aruba (Neth.)
Curaçao (Neth.)
Coro
Maracaibo
Barquisimeto
Caracas
Valencia
Maracay
Lake Maracaibo
Acarigua
Barinas
San Fernando de Apure
Ciudad Bolívar
R. Orinoco
Ciudad Guayana
El Tigre
Orinoco Delta
Embalse de Guri
El Callao
R. Tigre
VENEZUELA

Latitude/Longitude labels (bottom): 85° W, 80° W, 75° W, 70° W, 65° W
Map grid references (bottom): H, I, J, K, L

Inset: JAMAICA

Lucea
Montego Bay
Falmouth
St Ann's Bay
Oracabessa
Port Maria
Grange Hill
Negril
The Cockpit Country
Cambridge
Highgate
Annotto Bay
Port Antonio
South West Point
Savanna-la-Mar
Christiana
Don Figueroa Mts
Ewarton
Blue Mt Peak 2256
Lacovia
Chapelton
Bog Walk
Blue Mountains
Black River
Mandeville
May Pen
Spanish Town
Kingston
Bull Savannah
Morant Bay
Port Morant
Portland Bight
JAMAICA
Portland Point

Inset: TRINIDAD

VENEZUELA
Diego Martin
El Tucuche 936
Mt Aripo 940
Galera Point
Port of Spain
Tunapuna
Arima
Sangre Grande
Chaguanas
Trinidad
Gulf of Paria
Couva
Prince's Town
Rio Claro
San Fernando
Point Fortin
Penal
Siparia
Trinity Hills 304
Galeota Point

Inset: ST LUCIA

Pointe du Cap
ST LUCIA
Cap Marquis
Anse-la-Raye
Castries
Dennery
Mount Gimie 950
Soufrière
Micoud
Choiseul
Laborie
Vieux Fort

Scale : One centimetre on this map is the same as 200 kilometres on the ground.

0 200 400 600 800 1000 1200 km

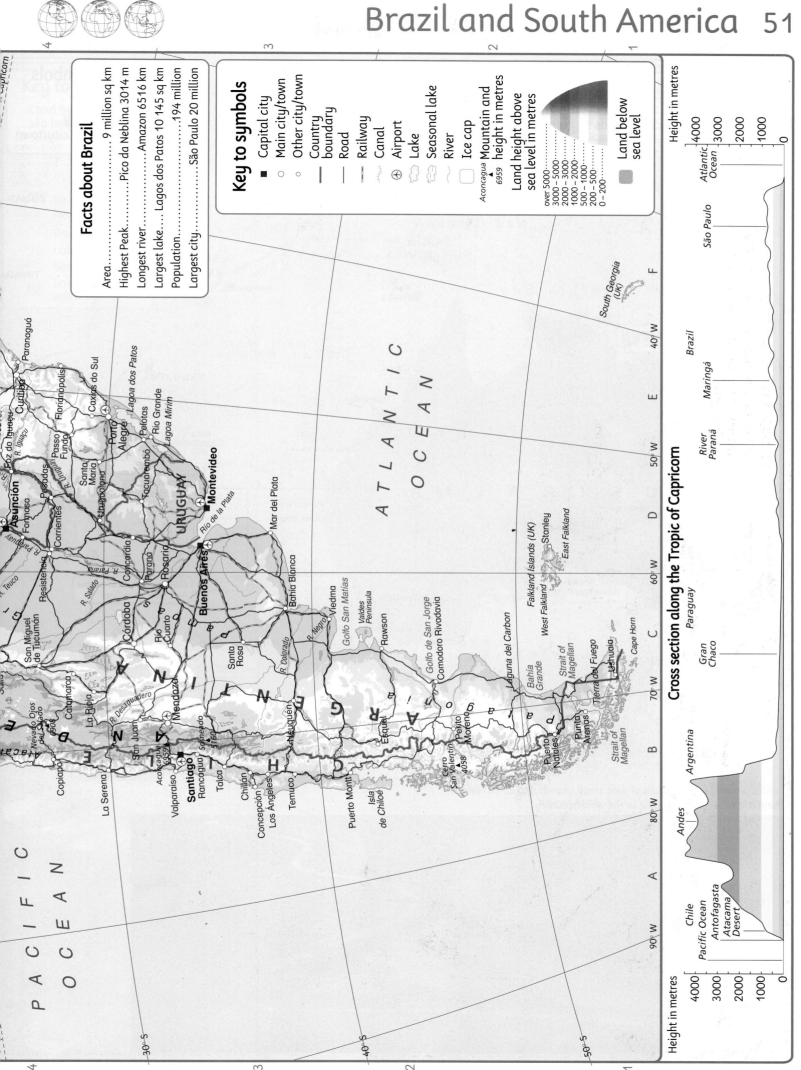

Facts about Brazil

Area..9 million sq km
Highest Peak............Pico da Neblina 3014 m
Longest river......................Amazon 6516 km
Largest lake.....Lagos dos Patos 10 145 sq km
Population.................................194 million
Largest city........................São Paulo 20 million

Key to symbols

■ Capital city
○ Main city/town
○ Other city/town
| Country boundary
| Road
| Railway
Canal
⊕ Airport
Lake
Seasonal lake
River
Ice cap
▲ *Aconcagua* Mountain and
  6959 height in metres

Land height above sea level in metres
over 5000
3000 – 5000
2000 – 3000
1000 – 2000
500 – 1000
200 – 500
0 – 200

Land below sea level

Cross section along the Tropic of Capricorn

Height in metres
4000
3000
2000
1000
0

Chile · Pacific Ocean · Antofagasta · Atacama Desert
Andes
Argentina
Gran Chaco
Paraguay
River Paraná
Maringá
Brazil
São Paulo
Atlantic Ocean

The Arctic Ocean is the smallest of the world's oceans. It is very cold and mostly covered with sea ice. In summer whales, seals and other creatures come to the Arctic Ocean looking for food.

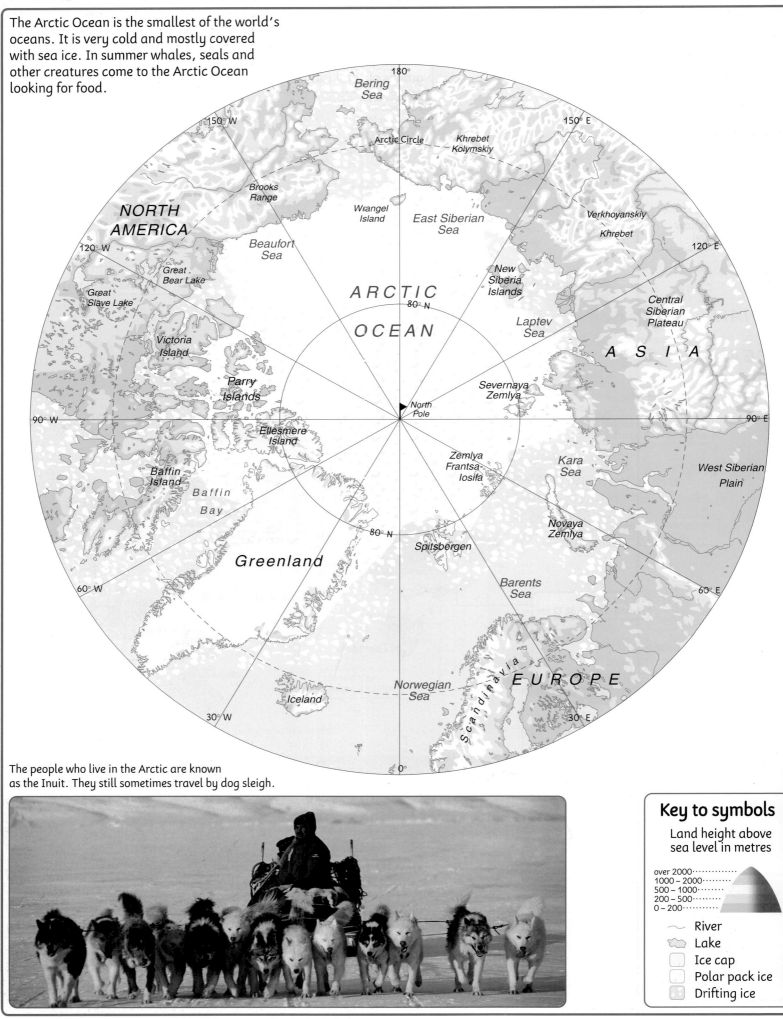

180°

Bering Sea

150° W

Arctic Circle

Khrebet Kolymskiy

150° E

Brooks Range

Wrangel Island

East Siberian Sea

Verkhoyanskiy Khrebet

NORTH AMERICA

Beaufort Sea

New Siberia Islands

120° E

120° W

Great Bear Lake

Laptev Sea

Central Siberian Plateau

Great Slave Lake

ARCTIC

80° N

A S I A

Victoria Island

OCEAN

Severnaya Zemlya

Parry Islands

90° W

90° E

Ellesmere Island

North Pole

Zemlya Frantsa-Iosifa

Kara Sea

West Siberian Plain

Baffin Island

Novaya Zemlya

Baffin Bay

80° N

60° W

Spitsbergen

Greenland

Barents Sea

60° E

Scandinavia

EUROPE

30° W

Norwegian Sea

30° E

Iceland

0°

The people who live in the Arctic are known as the Inuit. They still sometimes travel by dog sleigh.

Key to symbols

Land height above sea level in metres

over 2000
1000 – 2000
500 – 1000
200 – 500
0 – 200

~ River
Lake
Ice cap
Polar pack ice
Drifting ice

0   500   1000   1500   2000 km

Scale : One centimetre on this map is the same as 350 kilometres on the ground.

Names of bases numbered on map
① Comandante Ferraz (Brazil)
② King Sejong (South Korea)
③ Artigas (Uruguay)
④ Frei (Chile)
⑤ Bellingshausen (Russian Federation)
⑥ Great Wall (China)
⑦ Escudero (Chile)
⑧ Jubany (Argentina)
⑨ Arctowski (Poland)
⑩ O'Higgins (Chile)
⑪ San Martin (Argentina)

Antarctica is the world's coldest, driest and windiest continent. It is covered by a thick sheet of ice. In many places the ice is thicker than the highest mountains in the UK. Very few plants and animals survive here.

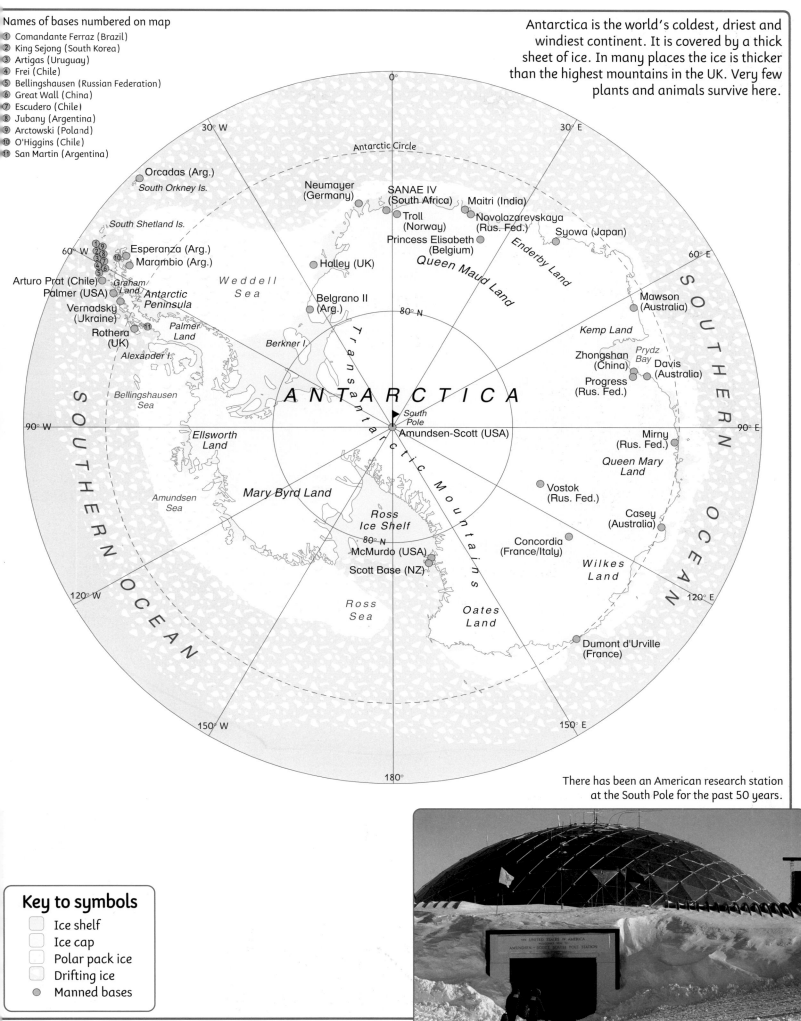

There has been an American research station at the South Pole for the past 50 years.

Key to symbols

- Ice shelf
- Ice cap
- Polar pack ice
- Drifting ice
- ● Manned bases

500   1000   1500   2000 km

Scale : One centimetre on this map is the same as 350 kilometres on the ground.

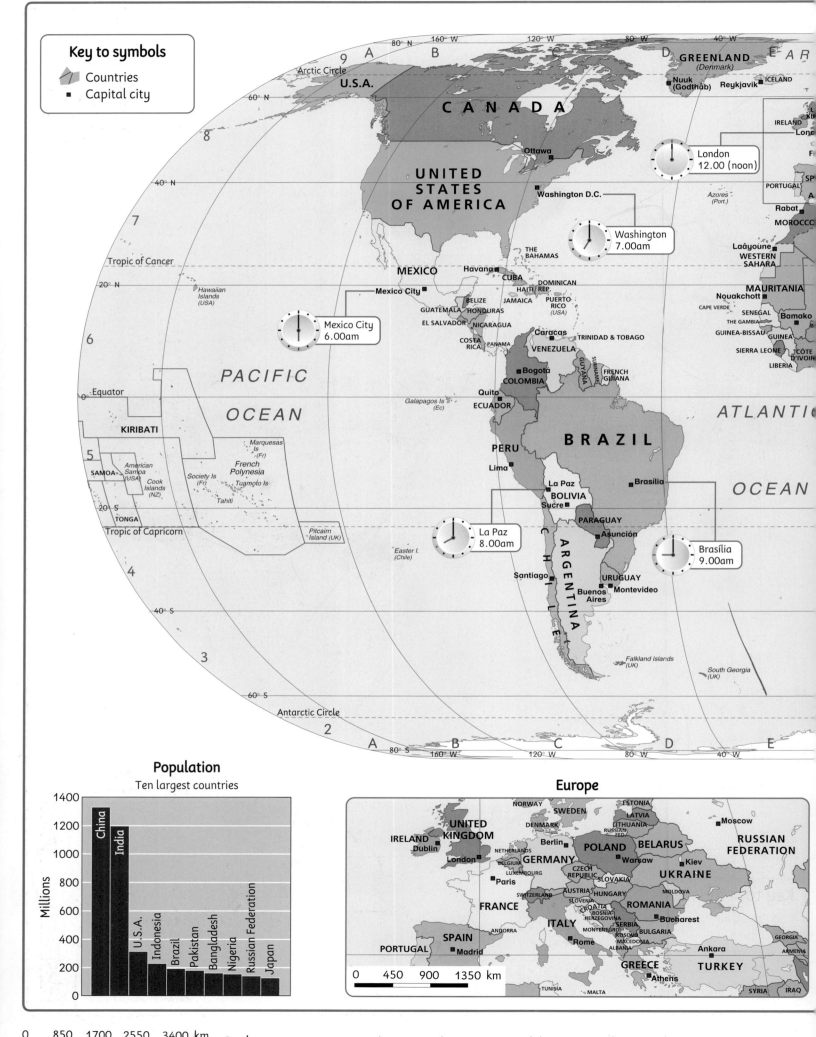

Key to symbols

Countries
■ Capital city

80° N   160° W   120° W   80° W   40° W
9 A   B   C   D   GREENLAND   E   A R
Arctic Circle   (Denmark)
9   Nuuk   ICELAND
                                    (Godthåb)   Reykjavik
60° N
U.S.A.
8   C A N A D A
40° N   IRELAND   Lonc
            Ottawa
7   UNITED
        STATES   Washington D.C.
        OF AMERICA   Azores   PORTUGAL   SP
                                            (Port.)   A
                        Washington   Rabat
Tropic of Cancer   7.00am   MOROCCO
20° N   Hawaiian   THE
        Islands   Havana   BAHAMAS   Laâyoune
        (USA)   MEXICO   CUBA   WESTERN
                        DOMINICAN   SAHARA
6   Mexico City   HAITI/ REP.
            Mexico City   PUERTO   MAURITANIA
            6.00am   GUATEMALA   RICO   Nouakchott
        Equator   EL SALVADOR   HONDURAS   (USA)   CAPE VERDE   SENEGAL
                        NICARAGUA   THE GAMBIA   Bamako
0   COSTA   Caracas   TRINIDAD & TOBAGO   GUINEA-BISSAU   GUINEA
PACIFIC   Galapagos Is   RICA   PANAMA   VENEZUELA   GUYANA   SIERRA LEONE   CÔTE
            (Ec)   Quito   GUYANA   FRENCH   D'IVOIRE
OCEAN   ECUADOR   COLOMBIA   SURINAME   GUIANA   LIBERIA
        KIRIBATI   Bogotá   ATLANTIC
5   B R A Z I L
    SAMOA   Marquesas   PERU
    American   Is
    Samoa   (Fr)   French   Lima   La Paz   Brasília   OCEAN
    (USA)   Society Is   Polynesia   BOLIVIA
    Cook   (Fr)   Tuamoto Is   Sucre   Brasília
    Islands   Tahiti   9.00am
    (NZ)   La Paz   PARAGUAY
20° S   TONGA   8.00am   Asunción
Tropic of Capricorn   Pitcairn   ARGENTINA   URUGUAY
            Island (UK)   Easter I.   Santiago   Buenos   Montevideo
                (Chile)   CHILE   Aires
4
40° S
3   Falkland Islands   South Georgia
                            (UK)   (UK)
60° S
Antarctic Circle
2 A   B   C   D   E
80° S
160° W   120° W   80° W   40° W

London
12.00 (noon)

Population
Ten largest countries

1400
1200
1000
800
600
400
200
0

China | India | U.S.A. | Indonesia | Brazil | Pakistan | Bangladesh | Nigeria | Russian Federation | Japan

Millions

Europe

NORWAY   SWEDEN   ESTONIA
                    LATVIA   Moscow
UNITED   DENMARK   LITHUANIA
KINGDOM   RUSSIAN   RUSSIAN
IRELAND   Berlin   FED.   FEDERATION
Dublin   NETHERLANDS   POLAND   BELARUS
London   BELGIUM   GERMANY   Warsaw   Kiev
    LUXEMBOURG   CZECH   UKRAINE
        Paris   REPUBLIC   SLOVAKIA
            SWITZERLAND   AUSTRIA   HUNGARY   MOLDOVA
    FRANCE   SLOVENIA   ROMANIA
            CROATIA   BOSNIA   Bucharest
            HERZEGOVINA   SERBIA   BULGARIA
        ITALY   MONTENEGRO   KOSOVO   GEORGIA
    SPAIN   ANDORRA   Rome   MACEDONIA   Ankara   ARMENIA
PORTUGAL   Madrid   ALBANIA   GREECE   TURKEY
                    Athens
            0   450   900   1350 km   TUNISIA   MALTA   SYRIA   IRAQ

0   850   1700   2550   3400 km

Scale : One centimetre on this map is the same as 850 kilometres on the ground.

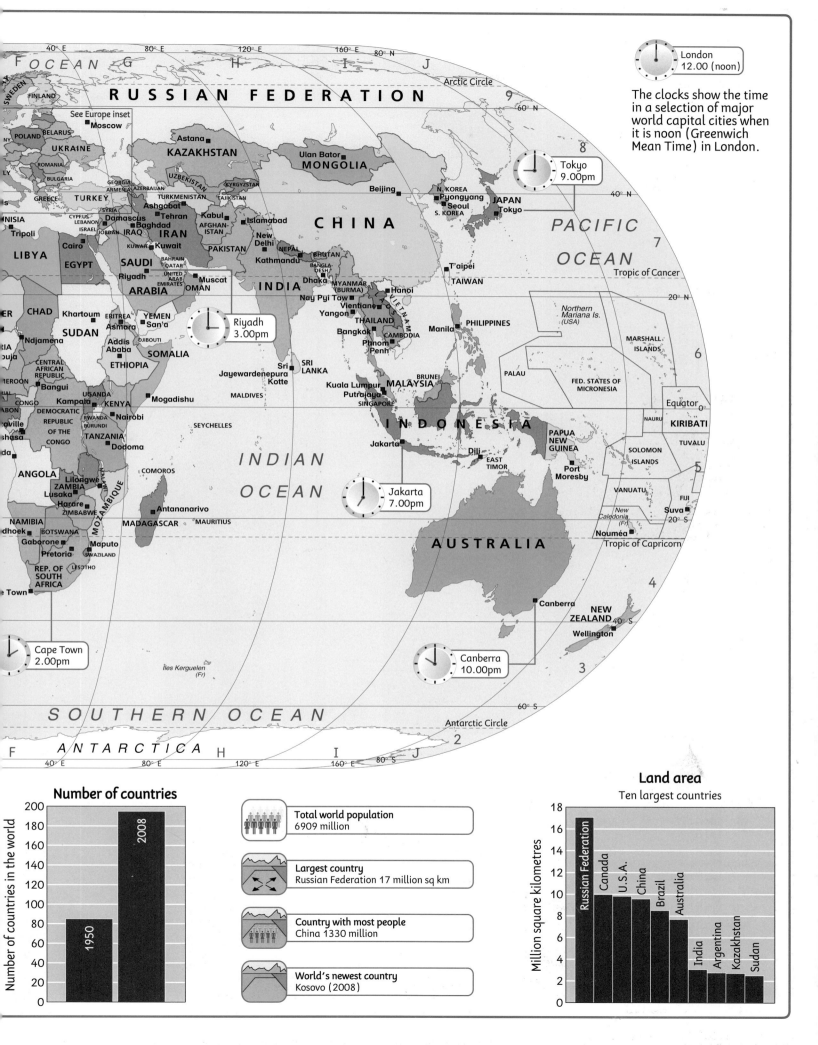

London
12.00 (noon)

The clocks show the time in a selection of major world capital cities when it is noon (Greenwich Mean Time) in London.

Tokyo
9.00pm

Riyadh
3.00pm

Jakarta
7.00pm

Canberra
10.00pm

Cape Town
2.00pm

OCEAN
SWEDEN
FINLAND
G
Arctic Circle
RUSSIAN FEDERATION
See Europe inset
Moscow
POLAND
BELARUS
UKRAINE
ROMANIA
BULGARIA
GEORGIA
ARMENIA AZERBAIJAN
GREECE
TURKEY
KAZAKHSTAN
Astana
UZBEKISTAN
TURKMENISTAN
KYRGYZSTAN
TAJIKISTAN
Ulan Bator
MONGOLIA
Beijing
N. KOREA
Pyongyang
Seoul
S. KOREA
JAPAN
Tokyo
60° N
40° N
9
8
CYPRUS
SYRIA
LEBANON
ISRAEL JORDAN
TUNISIA
Tripoli
Damascus
Ashgabat
Tehran
Baghdad
IRAQ
IRAN
Kabul
AFGHAN-
ISTAN
Islamabad
New
Delhi
CHINA
LIBYA
EGYPT
Cairo
KUWAIT
Kuwait
SAUDI
Riyadh
ARABIA
BAHRAIN
QATAR
UNITED
ARAB
EMIRATES
PAKISTAN
Muscat
OMAN
NEPAL
Kathmandu
BHUTAN
BANGLA-
DESH
Dhaka
INDIA
MYANMAR
(BURMA)
Nay Pyi Taw
Yangon
Hanoi
Vientiane
THAILAND
Bangkok
CAMBODIA
Phnom
Penh
T'aipei
TAIWAN
Manila
PHILIPPINES
PACIFIC
OCEAN
Tropic of Cancer
20° N
7
CHAD
Khartoum
ERITREA
Asmara
YEMEN
San'a
SUDAN
Ndjamena
DJIBOUTI
Addis
Ababa
SOMALIA
ETHIOPIA
Sri
Jayewardenepura
Kotte
SRI
LANKA
MALDIVES
BRUNEI
Kuala Lumpur
Putrajaya
SINGAPORE
MALAYSIA
Northern
Mariana Is.
(USA)
MARSHALL
ISLANDS
PALAU
FED. STATES OF
MICRONESIA
6
CENTRAL
AFRICAN
REPUBLIC
CAMEROON
Bangui
CONGO
UGANDA
Kampala
DEMOCRATIC
REPUBLIC
OF THE
CONGO
RWANDA
BURUNDI
KENYA
Nairobi
Mogadishu
SEYCHELLES
TANZANIA
Dodoma
INDONESIA
Jakarta
Dili
EAST
TIMOR
PAPUA
NEW
GUINEA
Port
Moresby
NAURU
KIRIBATI
TUVALU
SOLOMON
ISLANDS
Equator
0°
ANGOLA
ZAMBIA
Lilongwe
Lusaka
MALAWI
Harare
ZIMBABWE
MOZAMBIQUE
COMOROS
Antananarivo
MADAGASCAR
MAURITIUS
INDIAN
OCEAN
AUSTRALIA
VANUATU
New
Caledonia
(Fr)
Nouméa
FIJI
Suva
5
20° S
NAMIBIA
Windhoek
Gaborone
BOTSWANA
Pretoria
SWAZILAND
REP. OF
SOUTH
AFRICA
LESOTHO
Maputo
Cape Town
Tropic of Capricorn
Canberra
NEW
ZEALAND
Wellington
40° S
4
Îles Kerguelen
(Fr)
3
60° S
SOUTHERN OCEAN
Antarctic Circle
ANTARCTICA
80° S
2
40° E   80° E   120° E   160° E

40° E   80° E   120° E   160° E   80° N

Number of countries

Number of countries in the world

200
180
160
140
120
100
80
60
40
20
0

1950
2008

Total world population
6909 million

Largest country
Russian Federation 17 million sq km

Country with most people
China 1330 million

World's newest country
Kosovo (2008)

Land area
Ten largest countries

Million square kilometres

18
16
14
12
10
8
6
4
2
0

Russian Federation
Canada
U.S.A.
China
Brazil
Australia
India
Argentina
Kazakhstan
Sudan

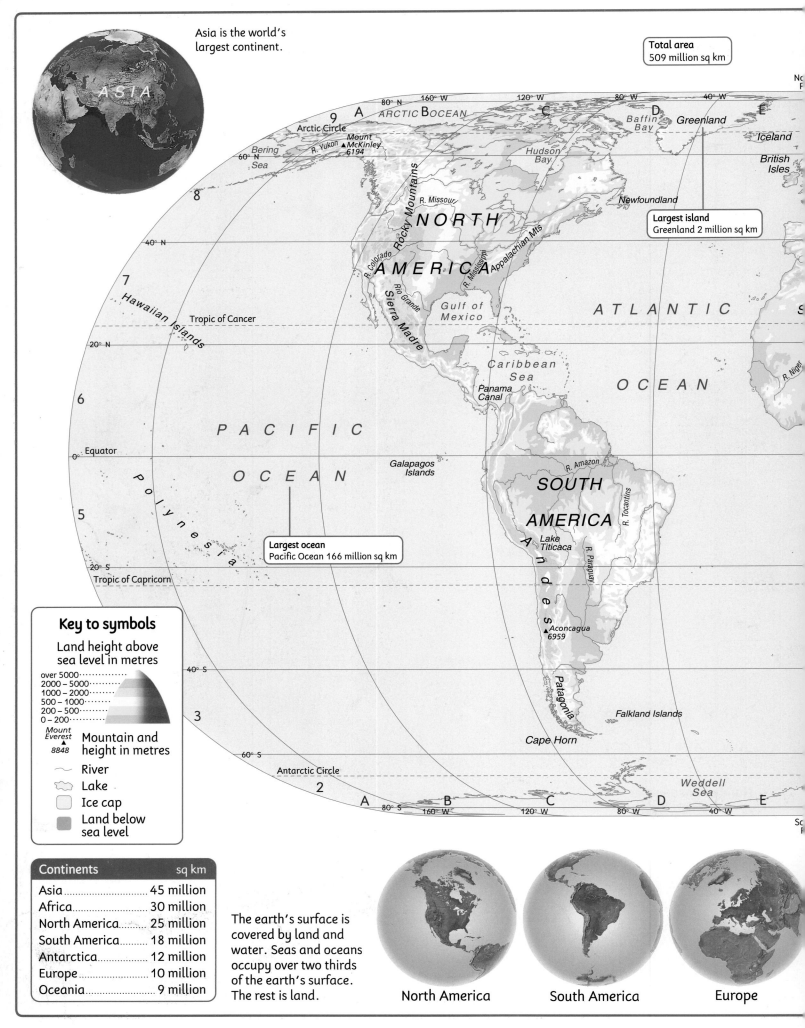

Asia is the world's largest continent.

ASIA

Total area
509 million sq km

Largest island
Greenland 2 million sq km

80° N   160° W   120° W   80° W   40° W

9 A   ARCTIC B OCEAN   C   D   E
Arctic Circle   Baffin Bay   Greenland   Iceland

60° N   R. Yukon   ▲ Mount McKinley 6194   Hudson Bay   British Isles
Bering Sea

8   R. Missouri   Newfoundland

NORTH

40° N   R. Colorado   Rocky Mountains

7   AMERICA   R. Mississippi   Appalachian Mts   A T L A N T I C

Hawaiian Islands   Sierra Madre   Rio Grande   Gulf of Mexico   O C E A N
Tropic of Cancer

20° N   R. Niger

Caribbean Sea

6   Panama Canal   O C E A N

P A C I F I C

Equator   Galapagos Islands   R. Amazon

0°   SOUTH   R. Tocantins
O C E A N

5   AMERICA
Largest ocean   Lake Titicaca
Pacific Ocean 166 million sq km   A   R. Paraguay
n
d
Polynesia   20° S   e   ▲ Aconcagua 6959
Tropic of Capricorn   s

Key to symbols

Land height above sea level in metres

over 5000
2000 – 5000
1000 – 2000
500 – 1000
200 – 500
0 – 200

40° S

Patagonia

3   Falkland Islands

Cape Horn

Mount Everest ▲ 8848   Mountain and height in metres

～ River

Lake

Ice cap

Land below sea level

60° S   Antarctic Circle

2   Weddell Sea

A   B   C   D   E
80° S   160° W   120° W   80° W   40° W

Continents	sq km
Asia	45 million
Africa	30 million
North America	25 million
South America	18 million
Antarctica	12 million
Europe	10 million
Oceania	9 million

The earth's surface is covered by land and water. Seas and oceans occupy over two thirds of the earth's surface. The rest is land.

North America   South America   Europe

0   850   1700   2550   3400 km

Scale : One centimetre on this map is the same as 850 kilometres on the ground.

The Pacific Ocean covers nearly half of the Earth.

PACIFIC OCEAN

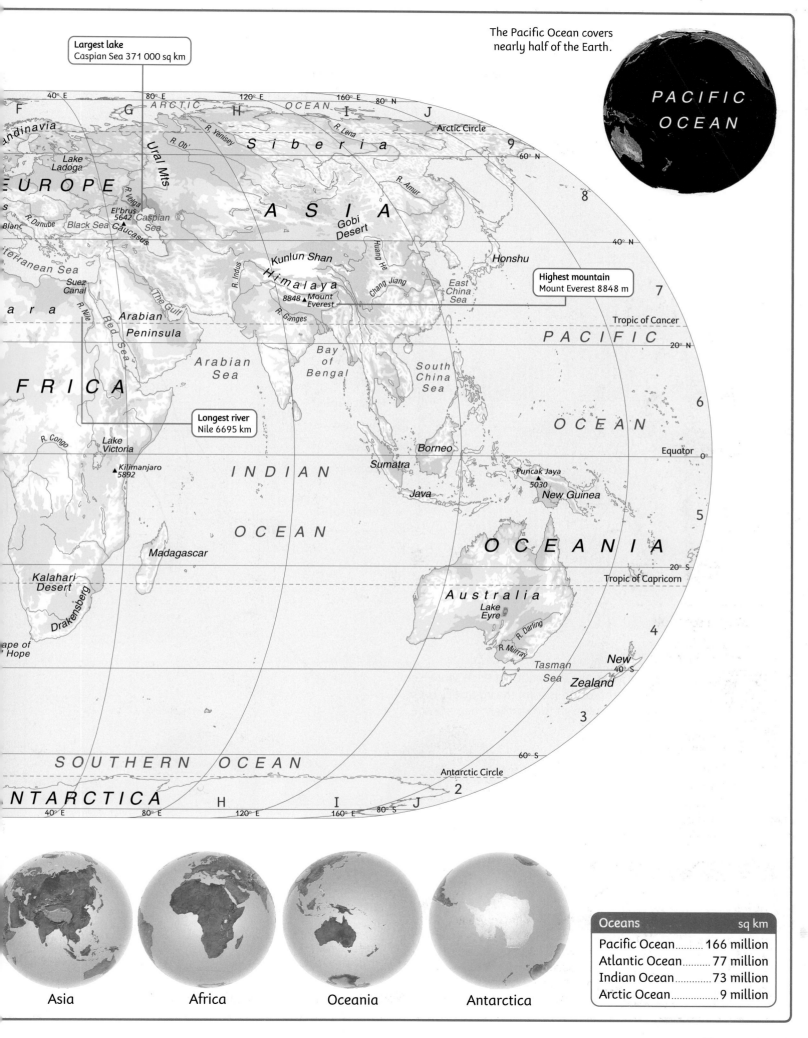

Largest lake
Caspian Sea 371 000 sq km

40° E   80° E   120° E   160° E   80° N

ARCTIC   OCEAN   Arctic Circle

Scandinavia   R. Yenisey   R. Lena

9

R. Ob'   Siberia

60° N

EUROPE   Ural Mts   8

Lake Ladoga   R. Volga   ASIA   R. Amur

El'brus 5642   Caspian Sea   Gobi Desert

Mt Blanc   R. Danube   Black Sea   Caucasus

40° N

Mediterranean Sea   Kunlun Shan   Honshu

Suez Canal   Himalaya   Huang He   **Highest mountain**
Mount Everest 8848 m   7

R. Nile   The Gulf   8848 ▲ Mount Everest   Chang Jiang   East China Sea

Sahara   Arabian Peninsula   R. Indus   R. Ganges   Tropic of Cancer

Red Sea   20° N

Arabian Sea   Bay of Bengal   PACIFIC

AFRICA   South China Sea

Longest river
Nile 6695 km   6

OCEAN

R. Congo   Lake Victoria   Borneo

Equator   0°

Kilimanjaro 5892   INDIAN   Sumatra   Puncak Jaya 5030

Java   New Guinea

5

Madagascar   OCEAN   OCEANIA

20° S

Kalahari Desert   Tropic of Capricorn

Drakensberg   Australia

Lake Eyre   4

Cape of Good Hope   R. Darling

R. Murray   New

Tasman   40° S

Sea   Zealand

3

60° S

SOUTHERN OCEAN   Antarctic Circle

2

ANTARCTICA   H   I   J   80° S

40° E   80° E   120° E   160° E

Asia   Africa   Oceania   Antarctica

Oceans	sq km
Pacific Ocean	166 million
Atlantic Ocean	77 million
Indian Ocean	73 million
Arctic Ocean	9 million

Climate graphs

The red line shows average temperature.
The blue bars show average monthly rainfall.

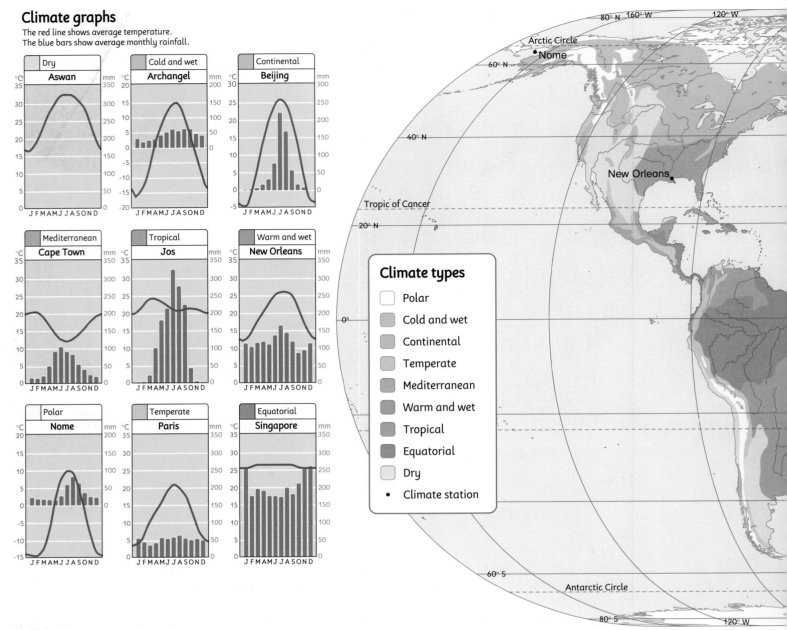

Seasons across the World

The year is divided into seasons. The length of each season can vary depending on how far a place is from the equator. These dials show the pattern of seasons in the northern hemisphere.

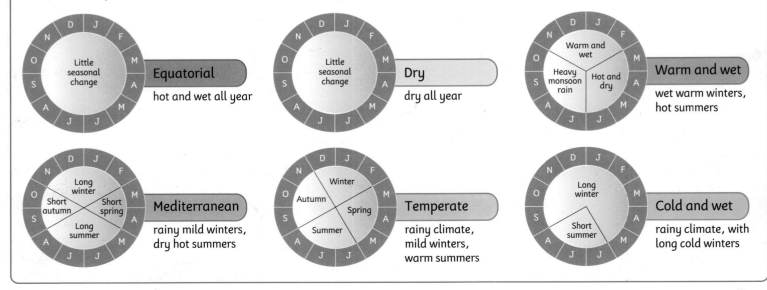

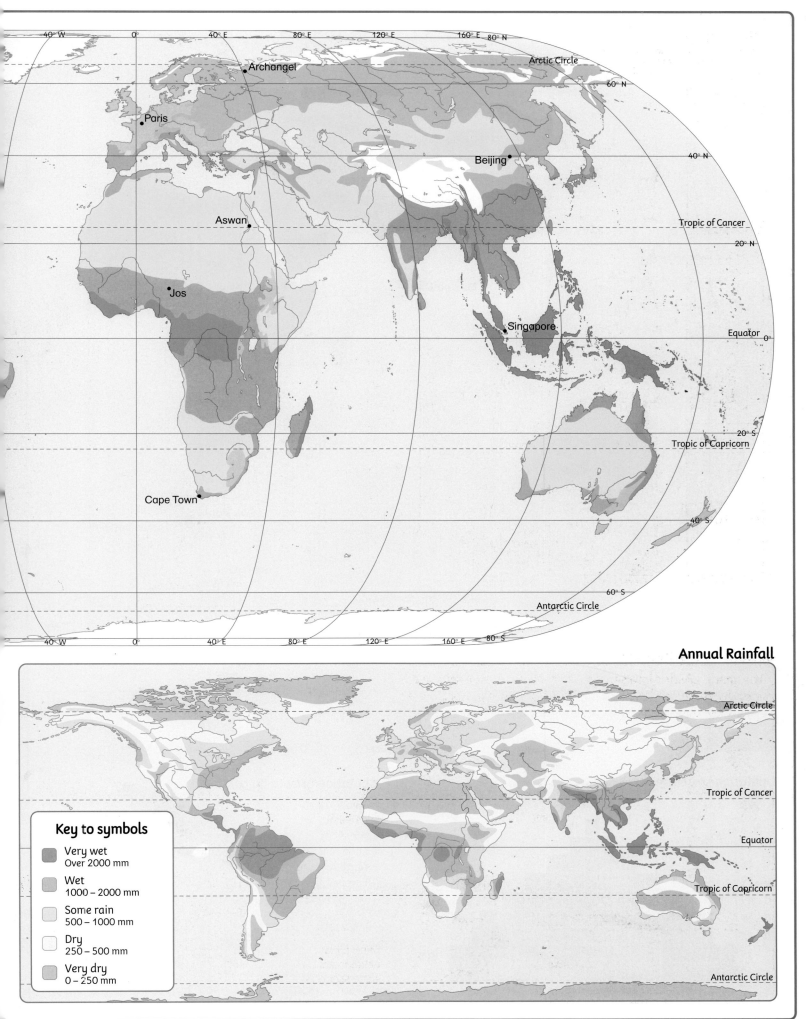

40° W   0°   40° E   80° E   120° E   160° E   80° N

Arctic Circle

60° N

Archangel

Paris

40° N

Beijing

Aswan

Tropic of Cancer

20° N

Jos

Singapore

Equator 0°

20° S

Tropic of Capricorn

Cape Town

40° S

60° S

Antarctic Circle

40° W   0°   40° E   80° E   120° E   160° E   80° S

Annual Rainfall

Arctic Circle

Tropic of Cancer

Equator

Tropic of Capricorn

Antarctic Circle

Key to symbols

- **Very wet** Over 2000 mm
- **Wet** 1000 – 2000 mm
- **Some rain** 500 – 1000 mm
- **Dry** 250 – 500 mm
- **Very dry** 0 – 250 mm

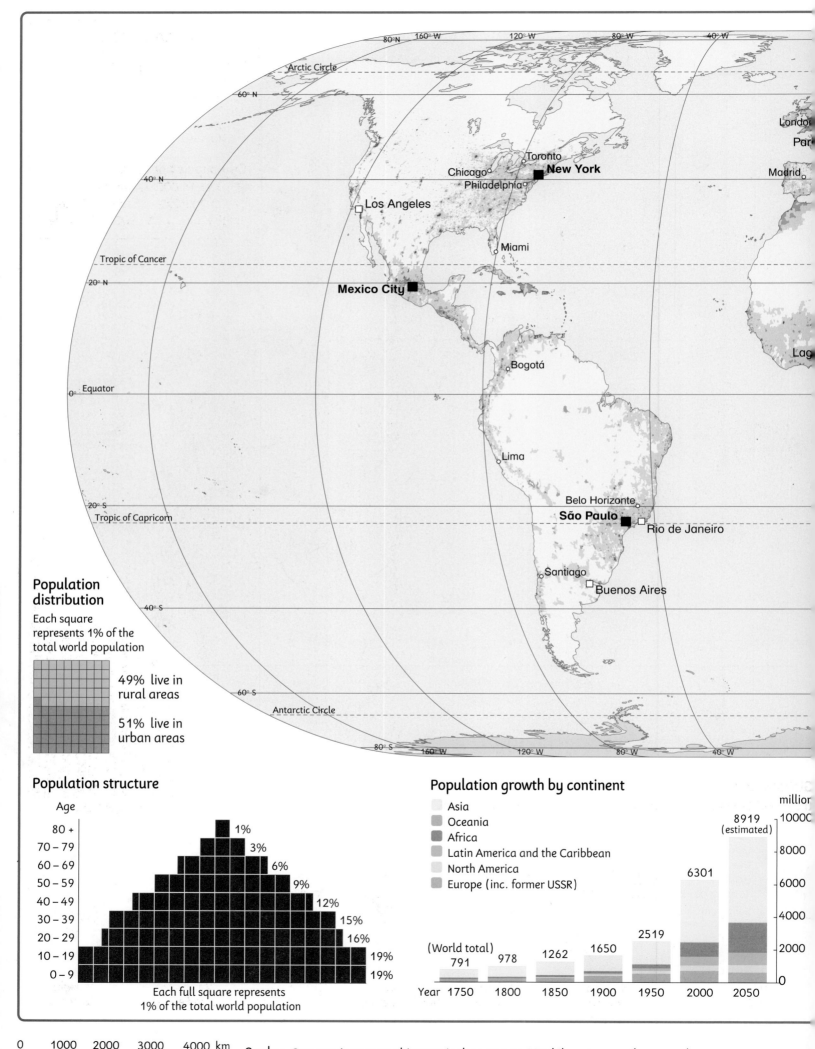

Population distribution

Each square represents 1% of the total world population

49% live in rural areas

51% live in urban areas

Population structure

Age

80 + — 1%
70 – 79 — 3%
60 – 69 — 6%
50 – 59 — 9%
40 – 49 — 12%
30 – 39 — 15%
20 – 29 — 16%
10 – 19 — 19%
0 – 9 — 19%

Each full square represents 1% of the total world population

Population growth by continent

million

Asia
Oceania
Africa
Latin America and the Caribbean
North America
Europe (inc. former USSR)

(World total)

Year	1750	1800	1850	1900	1950	2000	2050
	791	978	1262	1650	2519	6301	8919 (estimated)

Scale : One centimetre on this map is the same as 850 kilometres on the ground.

0   1000   2000   3000   4000 km

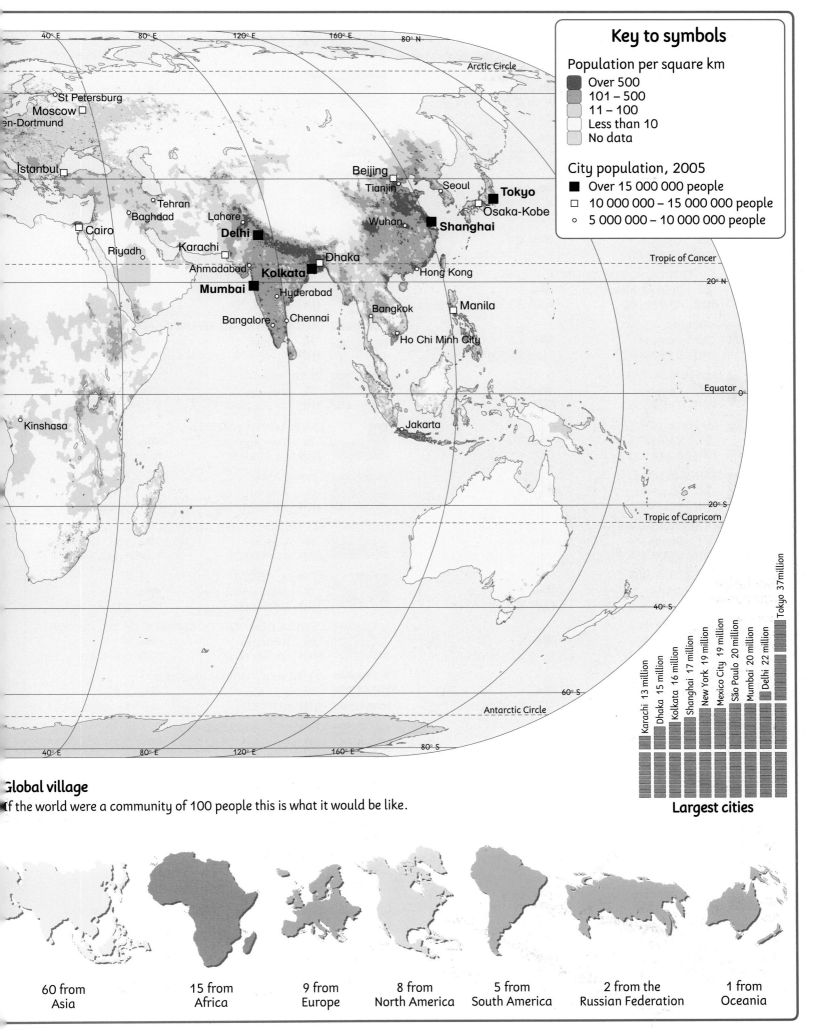

Key to symbols

Population per square km
- Over 500
- 101 – 500
- 11 – 100
- Less than 10
- No data

City population, 2005
- ■ Over 15 000 000 people
- □ 10 000 000 – 15 000 000 people
- ○ 5 000 000 – 10 000 000 people

40° E   80° E   120° E   160° E   80° N   Arctic Circle

St Petersburg
Moscow
en-Dortmund
İstanbul
Cairo
Tehran
Baghdad
Lahore
Riyadh
Karachi
Ahmadabad
Delhi
Kolkata
Mumbai
Hyderabad
Bangalore
Chennai
Beijing
Tianjin
Seoul
Tokyo
Osaka-Kobe
Wuhan
Shanghai
Dhaka
Hong Kong
Bangkok
Manila
Ho Chi Minh City
Jakarta
Kinshasa

Tropic of Cancer
20° N
Equator 0°
20° S
Tropic of Capricorn
40° S
60° S
Antarctic Circle
80° S

40° E   80° E   120° E   160° E

Largest cities

Karachi 13 million
Dhaka 15 million
Kolkata 16 million
Shanghai 17 million
New York 19 million
Mexico City 19 million
São Paulo 20 million
Mumbai 20 million
Delhi 22 million
Tokyo 37 million

Global village
If the world were a community of 100 people this is what it would be like.

60 from Asia

15 from Africa

9 from Europe

8 from North America

5 from South America

2 from the Russian Federation

1 from Oceania

Flag	COUNTRY, CONTINENT		
	🏛 Capital City 👥 Population	👣 Ecological footprint* ▱ Area (square km)	

AFGHANISTAN, ASIA — Kabul — 28 150 000 — n/a — 652 225 sq km

ALBANIA, EUROPE — Tiranë — 3 155 000 — 2.6 — 28 748 sq km

ALGERIA, AFRICA — Algiers — 34 895 000 — 1.9 — 2 381 741 sq km

ANGOLA, AFRICA — Luanda — 18 498 000 — 0.9 — 1 246 700 sq km

ARGENTINA, SOUTH AMERICA — Buenos Aires — 40 276 000 — 3 — 2 766 889 sq km

ARMENIA, ASIA — Yerevan — 3 083 000 — 1.6 — 29 800 sq km

AUSTRALIA, OCEANIA — Canberra — 21 293 000 — n/a — 7 692 024 sq km

AUSTRIA, EUROPE — Vienna — 8 364 000 — 4.9 — 83 855 sq km

BAHRAIN, ASIA — Manama — 791 000 — n/a — 691 sq km

BANGLADESH, ASIA — Dhaka — 162 221 000 — n/a — 143 998 sq km

BELARUS, EUROPE — Minsk — 9 634 000 — 4.2 — 207 600 sq km

BELGIUM, EUROPE — Brussels — 10 647 000 — 5.7 — 30 520 sq km

BENIN, AFRICA — Porto Novo — 8 935 000 — 1 — 112 620 sq km

BHUTAN, ASIA — Thimphu — 697 000 — n/a — 46 620 sq km

BOLIVIA, SOUTH AMERICA — La Paz/Sucre — 9 863 000 — 2.4 — 1 098 581 sq km

BOSNIA-HERZEGOVINA, EUROPE — Sarajevo — 3 767 000 — 3.4 — 51 130 sq km

BOTSWANA, AFRICA — Gaborone — 1 950 000 — 3.9 — 581 370 sq km

BRAZIL, SOUTH AMERICA — Brasília — 193 734 000 — n/a — 8 514 879 sq km

BRUNEI, ASIA — Bandar Seri Begawan — 400 000 — n/a — 5 765 sq km

BULGARIA, EUROPE — Sofia — 7 545 000 — 3.3 — 110 994 sq km

BURKINA FASO, AFRICA — Ouagadougou — 15 757 000 — 1.4 — 274 200 sq km

BURUNDI, AFRICA — Bujumbura — 8 303 000 — n/a — 27 835 sq km

CAMBODIA, ASIA — Phnom Penh — 14 805 000 — 0.9 — 181 035 sq km

CAMEROON, AFRICA — Yaoundé — 19 522 000 — 1.1 — 475 442 sq km

CANADA, NORTH AMERICA — Ottawa — 33 573 000 — 5.8 — 9 984 670 sq km

CENTRAL AFRICAN REPUBLIC, AFRICA — Bangui — 4 422 000 — 1.4 — 622 436 sq km

CHAD, AFRICA — Ndjamena — 11 206 000 — 1.8 — 1 284 000 sq km

CHILE, SOUTH AMERICA — Santiago — 16 970 000 — 3.1 — 756 945 sq km

CHINA, ASIA — Beijing — 1 330 265 000 — 1.8 — 9 584 492 sq km

COLOMBIA, SOUTH AMERICA — Bogotá — 45 660 000 — 1.9 — 1 141 748 sq km

CONGO, AFRICA — Brazzaville — 3 683 000 — 1 — 342 000 sq km

CONGO, DEMOCRATIC REPUBLIC OF THE, AFRICA — Kinshasa — 66 020 000 — 0.7 — 2 345 410 sq km

COSTA RICA, NORTH AMERICA — San José — 4 579 000 — 2.7 — 51 100 sq km

CÔTE D'IVOIRE, AFRICA — Yamoussoukro — 21 075 000 — 0.9 — 322 463 sq km

CROATIA, EUROPE — Zagreb — 4 416 000 — 3.3 — 56 538 sq km

CUBA, NORTH AMERICA — Havana — 11 204 000 — 2.3 — 110 860 sq km

CYPRUS, ASIA — Nicosia — 871 000 — n/a — 9 251 sq km

CZECH REPUBLIC, EUROPE — Prague — 10 369 000 — 5.3 — 78 864 sq km

DENMARK, EUROPE — Copenhagen — 5 470 000 — 7.2 — 43 075 sq km

*(global hectares per capita). Ecological footprints are a way of comparing consumption, lifestyle and environmental sustainability. High figures indicate high consumption, while low figures indicate greater sustainability. The world average is 1.8 gha per capita.

DJIBOUTI, AFRICA	Djibouti	0.9
	864 000	23 200 sq km
DOMINICAN REPUBLIC, NORTH AMERICA	Santo Domingo	1.4
	10 090 000	48 442 sq km
EAST TIMOR, ASIA	Dili	n/a
	1 134 000	14 874 sq km
ECUADOR, SOUTH AMERICA	Quito	1.9
	13 625 000	272 045 sq km
EGYPT, AFRICA	Cairo	1.4
	82 999 000	1 001 450 sq km
EL SALVADOR, NORTH AMERICA	San Salvador	n/a
	6 163 000	21 041 sq km
ERITREA, AFRICA	Asmara	0.8
	5 073 000	117 400 sq km
ESTONIA, EUROPE	Tallinn	6.4
	1 340 000	45 200 sq km
ETHIOPIA, AFRICA	Addis Ababa	n/a
	82 825 000	1 133 880 sq km
FINLAND, EUROPE	Helsinki	5.5
	5 326 000	338 145 sq km
FRANCE, EUROPE	Paris	4.6
	62 343 000	543 965 sq km
GABON, AFRICA	Libreville	n/a
	1 475 000	267 667 sq km
GEORGIA, ASIA	T'bilisi	n/a
	4 260 000	69 700 sq km
GERMANY, EUROPE	Berlin	4
	82 167 000	357 022 sq km
GHANA, AFRICA	Accra	1.6
	23 837 000	238 537 sq km
GREECE, EUROPE	Athens	5.8
	11 161 000	131 957 sq km
GUATEMALA, NORTH AMERICA	Guatemala City	1.7
	14 027 000	108 890 sq km
GUINEA, AFRICA	Conakry	1.5
	10 069 000	245 857 sq km
GUINEA-BISSAU, AFRICA	Bissau	1
	1 611 000	36 125 sq km
GUYANA, SOUTH AMERICA	Georgetown	n/a
	762 000	214 969 sq km

HAITI, NORTH AMERICA	Port-au-Prince	0.5
	10 033 000	27 750 sq km
HONDURAS, NORTH AMERICA	Tegucigalpa	2.2
	7 466 000	112 088 sq km
HUNGARY, EUROPE	Budapest	3.2
	9 993 000	93 030 sq km
ICELAND, EUROPE	Reykjavik	n/a
	323 000	102 820 sq km
INDIA, ASIA	New Delhi	0.8
	1 198 003 000	3 064 898 sq km
INDONESIA, ASIA	Jakarta	n/a
	229 965 000	1 919 445 sq km
IRAN, ASIA	Tehran	2.7
	74 196 000	1 648 000 sq km
IRAQ, ASIA	Baghdad	1.3
	30 747 000	438 317 sq km
IRELAND, EUROPE	Dublin	8.2
	4 515 000	70 282 sq km
ISRAEL, ASIA	Jerusalem	5.4
	7 170 000	20 770 sq km
ITALY, EUROPE	Rome	4.9
	59 870 000	301 245 sq km
JAMAICA, NORTH AMERICA	Kingston	n/a
	2 719 000	10 991 sq km
JAPAN, ASIA	Tokyo	4.1
	127 156 000	377 727 sq km
JORDAN, ASIA	Amman	2
	6 316 000	89 206 sq km
KAZAKHSTAN, ASIA	Astana	4.4
	15 637 000	2 717 300 sq km
KENYA, AFRICA	Nairobi	n/a
	39 802 000	582 646 sq km
KOSOVO, EUROPE	Pristina	n/a
	2 153 000	10 908 sq km
KUWAIT, ASIA	Kuwait	7.9
	2 985 000	17 818 sq km
KYRGYZSTAN, ASIA	Bishkek	1.3
	5 482 000	198 500 sq km
LAOS, ASIA	Vientiane	1
	6 320 000	236 800 sq km

LATVIA, EUROPE
Riga — 4.6
2 249 000 — 64 589 sq km

LEBANON, ASIA
Beirut — 2.1
4 224 000 — 10 452 sq km

LESOTHO, AFRICA
Maseru — n/a
2 067 000 — 30 355 sq km

LIBERIA, AFRICA
Monrovia — 1.2
3 955 000 — 111 369 sq km

LIBYA, AFRICA
Tripoli — 3.2
6 420 000 — 1 759 540 sq km

LITHUANIA, EUROPE
Vilnius — 3.3
3 287 000 — 65 200 sq km

LUXEMBOURG, EUROPE
Luxembourg — n/a
486 000 — 2 586 sq km

MACEDONIA (F.Y.R.O.M.), EUROPE
Skopje — n/a
2 042 000 — 25 713 sq km

MADAGASCAR, AFRICA
Antananarivo — 1.2
19 625 000 — 587 041 sq km

MALAWI, AFRICA
Lilongwe — n/a
15 263 000 — 118 484 sq km

MALAYSIA, ASIA
Kuala Lumpur/Putrajaya — n/a
27 468 000 — 332 965 sq km

MALI, AFRICA
Bamako — 1.9
13 010 000 — 1 240 140 sq km

MAURITANIA, AFRICA
Nouakchott — 3.1
3 291 000 — 1 030 700 sq km

MEXICO, NORTH AMERICA
Mexico City — 3.2
109 610 000 — 1 972 545 sq km

MOLDOVA, EUROPE
Chișinău — 1.7
3 604 000 — 33 700 sq km

MONGOLIA, ASIA
Ulan Bator — n/a
2 671 000 — 1 565 000 sq km

MONTENEGRO, EUROPE
Podgorica — n/a
624 000 — 13 812 sq km

MOROCCO, AFRICA
Rabat — 1.3
31 993 000 — 446 550 sq km

MOZAMBIQUE, AFRICA
Maputo — n/a
22 894 000 — 799 380 sq km

MYANMAR (BURMA), ASIA
Nay Pyi Taw/Yangon — 1
50 020 000 — 676 577 sq km

NAMIBIA, AFRICA
Windhoek — 3
2 171 000 — 824 292 sq km

NEPAL, ASIA
Kathmandu — n/a
29 331 000 — 147 181 sq km

NETHERLANDS, EUROPE
Amsterdam/The Hague — 4.6
16 592 000 — 41 526 sq km

NEW ZEALAND, OCEANIA
Wellington — 7.6
4 266 000 — 270 534 sq km

NICARAGUA, NORTH AMERICA
Managua — 2.3
5 743 000 — 130 000 sq km

NIGER, AFRICA
Niamey — 1.7
15 290 000 — 1 267 000 sq km

NIGERIA, AFRICA
Abuja — 1.6
154 729 000 — 923 768 sq km

NORTH KOREA, ASIA
Pyongyang — 1.4
23 906 000 — 120 538 sq km

NORWAY, EUROPE
Oslo — 4.2
4 812 000 — 323 878 sq km

OMAN, ASIA
Muscat — 3.5
2 845 000 — 309 500 sq km

PAKISTAN, ASIA
Islamabad — 0.7
180 808 000 — 803 940 sq km

PANAMA, NORTH AMERICA
Panama City — 3.2
3 454 000 — 77 082 sq km

PAPUA NEW GUINEA, OCEANIA
Port Moresby — 1.7
6 732 000 — 462 840 sq km

PARAGUAY, SOUTH AMERICA
Asunción — 3.4
6 349 000 — 406 752 sq km

PERU, SOUTH AMERICA
Lima — 1.8
29 165 000 — 1 285 216 sq km

PHILIPPINES, ASIA
Manila — n/a
91 983 000 — 300 000 sq km

POLAND, EUROPE
Warsaw — 3.9
38 074 000 — 312 683 sq km

PORTUGAL, EUROPE
Lisbon — 4.4
10 707 000 — 88 940 sq km

QATAR, ASIA
Doha — 9.7
1 409 000 — 11 437 sq km

ROMANIA, EUROPE
Bucharest — 2.7
21 275 000 — 237 500 sq km

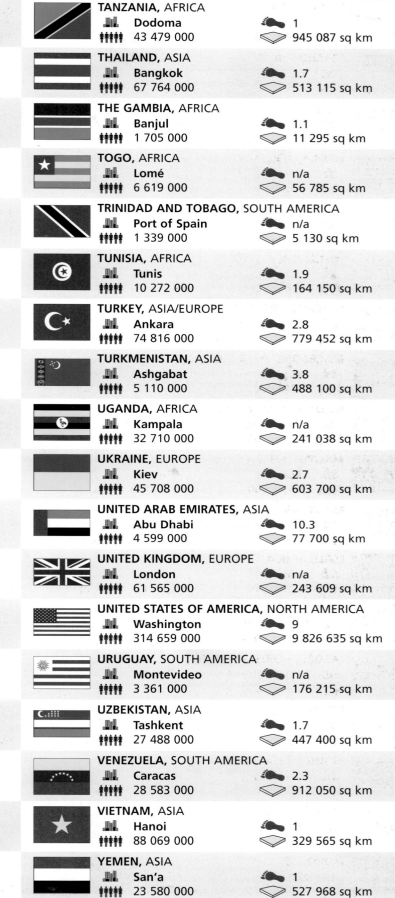

RUSSIAN FEDERATION, EUROPE/ASIA
Moscow · 4.4
140 874 000 · 17 075 400 sq km

SAUDI ARABIA, ASIA
Riyadh · 3.5
25 721 000 · 2 200 000 sq km

SENEGAL, AFRICA
Dakar · 1.2
12 534 000 · 196 720 sq km

SERBIA, EUROPE
Belgrade · n/a
7 335 000 · 77 453 sq km

SIERRA LEONE, AFRICA
Freetown · 0.8
5 696 000 · 71 740 sq km

SINGAPORE, ASIA
Singapore · 4.5
4 737 000 · 639 sq km

SLOVAKIA, EUROPE
Bratislava · 4.9
5 406 000 · 49 035 sq km

SLOVENIA, EUROPE
Ljubljana · 3.9
2 020 000 · 20 251 sq km

SOMALIA, AFRICA
Mogadishu · 1.5
9 133 000 · 637 657 sq km

SOUTH AFRICA, REPUBLIC OF, AFRICA
Pretoria/Cape Town · 2.7
50 110 000 · 1 219 090 sq km

SOUTH KOREA, ASIA
Seoul · 3.7
48 333 000 · 99 274 sq km

SPAIN, EUROPE
Madrid · 5.6
44 904 000 · 504 782 sq km

SRI LANKA, ASIA
Sri Jayewardenepura Kotte · 0.9
20 238 000 · 65 610 sq km

SUDAN, AFRICA
Khartoum · 2.2
42 272 000 · 2 505 813 sq km

SURINAME, SOUTH AMERICA
Paramaribo · n/a
520 000 · 163 820 sq km

SWAZILAND, AFRICA
Mbabane · n/a
1 185 000 · 17 364 sq km

SWEDEN, EUROPE
Stockholm · n/a
9 249 000 · 449 964 sq km

SWITZERLAND, EUROPE
Bern · 5.6
7 568 000 · 41 293 sq km

SYRIA, ASIA
Damascus · 1.6
21 906 000 · 185 180 sq km

TAJIKISTAN, ASIA
Dushanbe · 0.9
6 952 000 · 143 100 sq km

TANZANIA, AFRICA
Dodoma · 1
43 479 000 · 945 087 sq km

THAILAND, ASIA
Bangkok · 1.7
67 764 000 · 513 115 sq km

THE GAMBIA, AFRICA
Banjul · 1.1
1 705 000 · 11 295 sq km

TOGO, AFRICA
Lomé · n/a
6 619 000 · 56 785 sq km

TRINIDAD AND TOBAGO, SOUTH AMERICA
Port of Spain · n/a
1 339 000 · 5 130 sq km

TUNISIA, AFRICA
Tunis · 1.9
10 272 000 · 164 150 sq km

TURKEY, ASIA/EUROPE
Ankara · 2.8
74 816 000 · 779 452 sq km

TURKMENISTAN, ASIA
Ashgabat · 3.8
5 110 000 · 488 100 sq km

UGANDA, AFRICA
Kampala · n/a
32 710 000 · 241 038 sq km

UKRAINE, EUROPE
Kiev · 2.7
45 708 000 · 603 700 sq km

UNITED ARAB EMIRATES, ASIA
Abu Dhabi · 10.3
4 599 000 · 77 700 sq km

UNITED KINGDOM, EUROPE
London · n/a
61 565 000 · 243 609 sq km

UNITED STATES OF AMERICA, NORTH AMERICA
Washington · 9
314 659 000 · 9 826 635 sq km

URUGUAY, SOUTH AMERICA
Montevideo · n/a
3 361 000 · 176 215 sq km

UZBEKISTAN, ASIA
Tashkent · 1.7
27 488 000 · 447 400 sq km

VENEZUELA, SOUTH AMERICA
Caracas · 2.3
28 583 000 · 912 050 sq km

VIETNAM, ASIA
Hanoi · 1
88 069 000 · 329 565 sq km

YEMEN, ASIA
San'a · 1
23 580 000 · 527 968 sq km

ZAMBIA, AFRICA
Lusaka · 1.2
12 935 000 · 752 614 sq km

ZIMBABWE, AFRICA
Harare · 1
12 523 000 · 390 759 sq km

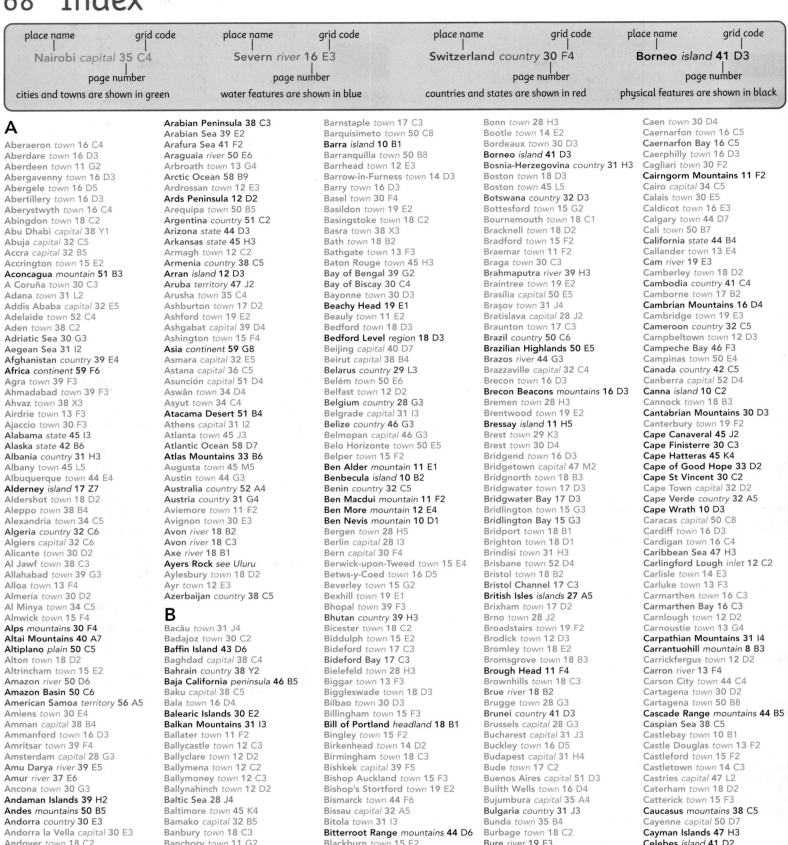

place name | grid code
Nairobi *capital* 35 C4
page number
cities and towns are shown in green

place name | grid code
Severn *river* 16 E3
page number
water features are shown in blue

place name | grid code
Switzerland *country* 30 F4
page number
countries and states are shown in red

place name | grid code
Borneo *island* 41 D3
page number
physical features are shown in black